rise above it

Complex problems have always been a part of life. To solve them, we must learn to rise above our everyday consciousness. We must rise to a new level, where the answers are waiting for us.

Other Books By Pavior Publishing:

The Violence Potential in Our Society by Ernest F. Pecci, M.D. ©1994 softcover, $9.95

Science and Human Transformation by William A. Tiller, PhD ©1997 softcover, $24.95

Conscience Acts of Creation by William A. Tiller, PhD; Walter E. Dibble, PhD; and Michael J. Kohane, PhD ©2001 softcover, $29.95

Chess: A Psychiatrist Matches Wits With Fritz by Ernest F. Pecci, Foreword by Garry Kasparov ©2001 hardcover, $24.95

A Sikh's Paradigm For Universal Peace by Meji Singh, PhD, Gyani ©2004 hardcover, $21.95

Guidance From Within by Ernest F. Pecci, M.D. ©2003 hardcover, $21.95

Visit our Website at www.Pavior.com

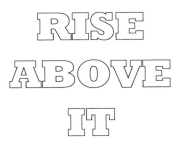

RISE ABOVE IT

A Psychiatrist Looks Within For a Higher Meaning to Life

Ernest F. Pecci, MD

Foreword by Elizabeth Kubler-Ross, MD

Pavior Publishing
Walnut Creek, California

Library of Congress Cataloging-in-Publication Data

Library of Congress Cataloging-in-Publication Data

Pecci, Ernest F.
  Rise above it : a psychiatrist looks within for a higher meaning to
life / Ernest F. Pecci ;
  foreword by Elizabeth Kubler-Ross.
    p. cm.
  ISBN 1-929331-09-6
  1. Meditation. I. Title.

BL627.P43 2005
204'.35--dc22
                                        2004021226

Dedication

In memory of Elizabeth Kubler-Ross, whose life
was a gift to me and to countless others.

Acknowledgements

My thanks to all of those who have encouraged me to share
these writings from my personal journals over the years.

I am grateful to Dr.Elizabeth Kubler-Ross for her years of
friendship, to Dr. Jack Holland, Dr. Robert Leichtman and
Dr. William Tiller for their continuing support. In addition
to his own influential writings, Dr. Holland has been an
inspirational speaker and instructor at San Jose State
University as well as at John F. Kennedy University in
Orinda, California. He also wrote the prologue to Dr.
William Tiller s groundbreaking book, *Science and Human
Transformation*, which Pavior published in 1997. With Carl
Japikse, Dr. Leichtman has published his own excellent
book, *The Act of Meditation* [Enthea Press, 1988], and
continues to conduct spiritual workshops in Big Sur,
California. He also provided me with the definition of *full
mind* that appears in the glossary to this book.

I would also like to express my appreciation to friends and
family members, including Joanne Walsh, Edward Sheppie,
Marguerite Kelley, and Eric La Brecque, who helped to
bring this book to its present form.

THIS BOOK WAS WRITTEN FOR YOU. Nothing happens by chance. The things you need for your next step in development are always placed, sometimes by a series of miraculous coincidences, into your hands.

You are ready now to lift up your eyes and to expand the vision and the awareness of your own nature and the nature of the world in which you live. Your mind is not limited to what you can see with your eyes. Neither is the value of you life limited to what you are now trying to accomplish.

Expanded perception comes only with the desire coupled with that mustard grain of faith that says, "There must be something more." It all begins to happen when you still the frantic mind and listen to the voice within that knows.

Spiritual development begins with the recognition that we are caught in a comic trap that consists of our accepting as reality the illusion of the material world. Far more serious is the loss of our own identity as we become caught up with survival fear in our dealings with others. As we grow, we become cloaked with personality, a very limited and limiting caricature of our true being. And as we lose sight of ourself we become closed off to God, the Indwelling Self.

Finally, something happens in the lives of many of us which compels an inner search. And once a sincere attempt is made to reestablish contact with the Indwelling Self, we are usually rewarded by enough initial success to encourage us to continue further. Progress is sometimes difficult to measure and we must persevere on faith to overcome the tendency to become discouraged.

Deep within the recesses of the mind, beyond the screen of visual imagery and the noisy inner dialogue of the mind to the Source of consciousness itself, resides the kindly voice, soft as the faint rustling of leaves on a warm summer night. It is the Eternal Self, the Indwelling Presence, The Transcendental Being with whom we shall one day reunite.

Once we have begun to listen, we have taken the first vital step. Everything else comes from this. We must take the time necessary to listen and to make this an important priority in our lives.

We must dare to see the limitations of our consciousness in a material body, and the weaknesses that hold us there. We must learn to grow beyond survival fear and to avoid becoming discouraged by knowing that we are not alone, and that all help is available for the asking.

We are never alone. God's attention is always focused upon us. Everyone is unique in some way, and everything we experience has been especially arranged for our own learning and greater development.

The Power of Silence

When, in meditation, as you sink into the quiet of your being, you enter the Great Silence. This silence is not merely a cessation of worldly clatter or the extinction of phantom images. This Silence is God at work, God in action.

Although the Presence is ever within your being, its effectiveness is hampered by your mental activity, to the extent that you keep your thinking machinery in operation. The greatest deterrent to spiritual growth is thinking. Keep this in mind as you think your way through your day.

When you have ceased to think and struggle, when you have reduced your inner turbulence to a quiet ripple of barely perceptible activity, you are close to the very presence and power of God.

The most significant advance toward interior silence occurs when you no longer need to deny error or to affirm truth. Then you will discover that an enormous lot of noise has been removed from your head. The game of right and wrong, the concepts of better and worse, big and small, rich and poor—all of these are the creators of noise in your head.

When all inner activity ceases, a sweet and blissful peace will descend upon you. And when you are immersed in this Great Silence and Peace, you will have become imbued with the power of God. This is the place where real healing occurs. This is the point where your higher level of consciousness can touch a friend who is in need, and lift him for a brief moment to a higher vibration. His "illness" cannot co-exist with God, for there is only one Power. Thus, he is healed.

Interior silence cannot be learned, nor can it be acquired by disciplines or through seeking. The Silence is always there; we have to learn to uncover it. If you could experience total Silence, you would be in heaven.

By a student, Don Wells

Table of Contents

Foreword 17

Introduction 19

Part 1

The reality of the Indwelling Presence. A basic understanding of the nature of God and His personal interest in us. On choosing the right path and protecting one's newborn faith.

The Practice of Seeing God 28

Making Contact in Meditation 29

Let Your Awareness Grow With Patience 30

Remembering God's Closeness in Childhood 31

On Finding the Right Path 32

Finding God's Face in Every Mirror 33

God Is A Personal God 34

Take Time to Receive God's Love 35

Learn To Listen 36

Gratitude Accompanies the Discovery of Self 37

Believe in God's Presence 38

On Trusting Your Initial Impulse 39
Self Pride Closes the Ears 41

Part 2

Encouragement to overcome the barriers of guilt and feelings of unworthiness which increase with the growing awareness of our weaknesses. The building of faith to persist, despite a seeming lack of progress in the absence of God's presence.

Each Has Talents According To His Needs 44

Advice When Progress Becomes Difficult 45

Take the Necessary Pause for Attunement 47

Approaching God as an Innocent Child 48

On Overcoming Weariness 49

The Causes of Tension 50

The Importance of Making a Beginning 51

Do Not Be Discouraged By Weaknesses 52

On Correcting Past Errors 53

Strive For Self-Acceptance 54

Each Day Is a Mini-Life of Its Own 55

On Rising Above the Opinions of Others 56

And Why Do You Doubt God's Love? 57

The Personal Nature of God's Caring 58

Protecting Your New-Born Faith 59

Take the Time to Ask for Help 60

Learn To Free the Future from Your Past 61

Appreciating the Value of Prayer 62

As You Believe So It Is! 63

Cultivate the Attitude of Sincerity 64

Part 3

The cultivation of Right Thinking. The concept of Maturity and Responsibility and the development of Right Attitude.

Purity of Heart 68

On Humility 69

Self-Pride Closes the Ears to Learning 70

Overcoming the Resistance to Praying 71

Control of the Tongue Through Right Thinking 72

On the Attitude of Respect 73

On Maturity 74

The Man of God is Never a Revolutionary 76

On Loneliness and Depression 77

On Seeking God's Love 78

Freedom Comes Through Surrendering 79

On Learning the Lesson of Surrender 80

Overcoming Apprehensions About the Future 81

Part 4

Rules and right practices to maintain progress and for conducting a wholesome and satisfying life. The application of these to one's daily relationships with family, acquaintances and colleagues.

Selfishness is the First Barrier to Overcome 84
Spiritual Growth Begins By Valuing Self and Family 85
How to Avoid Needless Suffering 87
The Greatest Challenge is Within Your Own Home 88
Kindness is God Working Through You 89
Seek to Know Your True Responsibilities 90
Communication Begins Wiith Listening 91
Judgment is a Barrier to Learning 92
Bring to Others a Joyful Attitude 93
Use Giving as a Way of Receiving 94
Accept Your Role in Controversial Situations 95
On Being Firm Rather Than Self-Righteous 96
Never Envy the Talents of Others 97
Avoid Rehearsing Arguments in Your Head 98

Part 5

The development of the will and the overcoming of the lower self. Understanding the nature of the battle within. A basic understanding of the ways of the world and of the mind, leading to a gradual change in perspective and a shifting of priorities to those things that are in attunement with the universal harmony of all things.

The Triune Nature of Man 103
On Seeking God's Presence Within 104
On the Nature of the Ego 105
How One Might Escape the Influence of the Ego 106
God's Love Overcomes Fear 107
How Man Swerves From the Path 108
The Lie of False Personality 110
Development of the Will 111
The Raising of Consciousness 112
Everything You Experience Originates Within 113
Live Each Day As If It Were Your Last 114
On Time and Its Proper Use 115
Everything is in a Constant State of Change 116
Let Your Will Schedule Your Mind 117
See Life as a Twice-Told Tale 118
Space and the Movements of Man Within It 119
The Rules for Attainment 121
Raise the Vibrations of Your Emotions to Love 122

Focus Your Awareness Upon Love 123
Seek to Live In Divine Presence 124
The Pathos of Man 125

Epilogue 127

Glossary 133

Foreword

My friendship with Dr. Ernest Pecci dates back to the early 1970's when I heard him speak before a large professional group of therapists at John F. Kennedy University in Orinda, California. I later attended his weekend workshop on "Psycho-spiritual Integration" which resonated to many of my own spiritual insights regarding the true nature of a human being and the need for all of us to help each other through the often painful journey of three-dimensional existence. The weekend offered us several pleasant opportunities to discuss our work and our dreams. The world was young then, and neither of us had any idea of the many challenge that lay ahead.

During our private conversations, we shared some of our personal spiritual experiences. We found many, often striking, similarities and took away renewed encouragement to use along our individual journeys. One of the many things I shared was a photograph I had taken of some beautiful scenery that showed a tall figure standing in the foreground like a powerful spiritual guide. My husband, at that time, chided me for having taken a double exposure. However, this was a camera in which the film automatically advanced after each picture was taken, making a double exposure virtually impossible. There are many things we cannot explain by the laws of physics, and that is because the forces that hold the universe in balance cannot be processed by our rational minds. However, we can often sense or experience these forces at higher levels of consciousness during the practice of meditation.

Dr. Pecci shared with me the beautiful thoughts that came to him during the course of his daily practice of meditation. I found them to be fascinating. That evening I had a strong premonition that this valuable collection of meditative insights was in danger of being lost in a fire. The next day, I asked him to give to me a copy of his current collection for safekeeping. Years later, these were, indeed, burned in a fire—but it was in my own home.

On October 6, 1994, my house in Virginia was burned to the ground by an angry neighbor who objected to my plans to house HIV-infected babies there. I was in a state of shock as I watched it burn, and with it everything that I owned. I had to keep reminding myself: "Everything happens for a purpose," and, "Adversity only makes you stronger." The three-dimensional world is definitely a lesson in dealing with loss. Life, at its best, is a painful learning experience. The more you learn, the harder it becomes, and the more you benefit from turning to a higher power to help you through the most difficult lessons. Learn to get in touch with the silence within yourself, and know that everything in this life has a purpose. There are no mistakes, no coincidences; all events are blessings given to us to learn from.

Elizabeth Kubler-Ross, May 2004

Introduction

Meditation for the Western World

Meditation has become a word in common usage in the Western world during the past thirty years, and many people now claim to practice it on occasion. There have been many studies confirming that the practice of meditation, even by the beginner, has a quieting effect upon the nervous system, a relaxation of pulse and blood pressure, and a feeling of being more "centered" and a sense of peacefulness. This would make you expect that meditation could easily become a self-reinforcing practice. Yet, I commonly hear, "I'm too busy to do it very often these days." I believe that when you understand the full value of the practice of meditation, that you will make it a much higher priority in your life.

Meditation is different from prayer in that in prayer we are extending our energies outward to God for help in lightening the burden of our earthly problems, while the purpose of meditation is to gain remembrance and attunement with God, and to realize our oneness with Him.

If you are unhappy with the way your life is going, you may have found that you cannot improve it with your rational mind alone. Rather, you must raise your consciousness above your problems of the day, to see it all from a new perspective. You can only do this through meditation. Meditation is more than just relaxation. Meditation is the act of opening oneself up to the flow of higher spiritual energies so as to heighten the vibration of both the mind and the body. It is an opening up to the experience of Presence, of Oneness with what we call God. There is no better way to fill our loneliness. There is no other way to reduce our fears. There is no other lasting way to dissolve our anger and our jealousies. This is the only way to be truly happy and to find inner peace.

Communicating with your Higher Self or God is not as difficult as you may have been led to believe. Your right brain, when relaxed and receptive, is capable of spontaneously attuning to a higher level of intuition and knowing. It merely requires stilling the chatter of the surface mind to open a space for the receptivity of "spiritual wisdom." There is nothing mysterious or mystical about it. Since all Mind is one, your consciousness must also be one with God consciousness. All that stands in your way is your barrier of fear and doubt. All that is needed now is desire and persistence to gradually restore your receptivity and trust toward an expanded sense of self.

Regardless of a lack of previous knowledge, you can begin this moment without extensive training. And the more you turn to it, the more open becomes this channel. Most wonderful is its constant availability. Fifteen minutes is enough in the beginning. Gradually, it may feel so pleasant that you might want to extend the time. Time spent thinking about God is never wasted, even if only for five minutes at different intervals during the day. And smiling, every time you think of God, is a great mood elevator.

When I first decided to meditate, I prepared a small room in my home that would be completely quiet when I closed the door. Then I sat upon the carpeted floor with my back held straight against one wall. I crossed my legs, closed my eyes and just waited with my ears open. It's as simple as that. I didn't know what I was waiting for, but my mind and my ears remained very alert. I placed my point of consciousness between my two eyes, as if searching with curiosity and with no pressure of time. The quiet waiting, of itself, felt so pleasant that I sometimes extended the time to an hour or more without realizing how much time had gone by.

After a period of practicing this exercise for several weeks, I began receiving inspirational thoughts that I began to write down in a daily journal. Often the ideas would be associated with a tingling on the top of my head, but not always. It is these thoughts that I am sharing here in their natural progression. Only much later did I read books available on the art of meditation. But by then I realized that all I really needed to know was the phrase: "Let go and let God." Let God's love flow through you without resistance!

During meditation, messages generally come to me as feeling/thoughts that I try to put into words. Often, from this level, the thoughts appear so obvious that I do not see the necessity of writing them down.

However, upon reviewing them at a later date, I find that they contain a simple wisdom that is beyond my normal state of thinking/consciousness.

It is usually helpful to begin each session with a brief prayer. If your mind is troubled by worries and responsibilities you might spend a few minutes putting your list of problems into God's hands. Then, let go of them and begin to listen. The initial goal is to learn to control your mind to stop its incessant chatter. This can best be done by listening very intently as if you truly believed that God is quietly whispering to you. For example, imagine that you were seated in a restaurant and heard some people at a nearby table whispering. If you were really interested in listening to what they were saying, you would not be distracted by extraneous thoughts.

As all random thinking subsides, you will be able to enter into the great silence. This is not a trance-like state but a state of heightened mental clarity and awareness that is receptive to whatever new thought or sensation comes in from a higher level to fill the void. It may seem, at times, as if nothing is happening. But something always does that will make you the better for it in subtle ways.

Remember, that once you begin the practice of meditation, you are helped and guided along the way. You may ask for help in relieving the common feelings of anger and fear which are impediments to stilling the mind. This will gradually come more easily with time. You cannot think about God for even five minutes without attaining some benefit.

As I described in my book, *Guidance From Within*, you may focus for awhile upon a particular problem and then begin writing down whatever thoughts occur to you about it. However, meditation is more than just a mechanism for intuitive problem-solving. It is a means by which you slowly raise your mental and physical vibration until, with time, you see yourself, your surroundings, and your life from a new perspective.

Just as an acorn that lies beneath the ground when properly watered grows into a mighty oak, so the pattern of perfection of oneness with God lies dormant within each of us, waiting for the right vibratory influences to unfold. All that this requires is simple listening with intent. The creative forces rise naturally up the proper channels. Our task is to remove that which hinders the flow. Negative or selfish thoughts hinder the flow. The love of God enhances the flow. The intention and the desire to make contact invites it. The connection to God or our Higher Self is a two-way process.

How much easier it becomes when you think of meditation as something you are doing together with God. Remember that God does most of the work once you have given Him your willingness. Each attempt increases the vibratory rate of your mind and body a seemingly insignificant amount. And constant practice, even for brief moments, with the right desire will eventually bring measurable results. What is the right desire?—just wanting to be with God.

Meditation, when properly practiced, is a powerful tool for enriching our lives. There is the feeling of being in touch with spirit and, with this, the gradual awakening of our mind to higher realms of awareness. Contact with God is far simpler to accomplish than is generally appreciated. It does not require the study of deep breathing, the chanting of mantras, or the study of yoga that was meant for a different culture and generation. (However, these practices still do have value if you are inclined to study them.) All that is essential is the belief, the desire, and the intent to make the contact. When accompanied with a sense of deep reverence and devotion there is a joyful opening of the heart.

Many of the beneficial results of meditation are rarely apparent during meditation, itself, but it gradually influences our conscious awareness and activities in the days following. There is a powerful accumulative effect to even brief periods of meditation. Meditation is attuning to the channel through which God is constantly broadcasting His love to you. You are always standing in the presence of God, but you are usually too distracted to notice.

Following are some of the benefits that you can expect from the daily practice of meditation:

1

A healing of the grief, guilt, regrets, and wounds in our subconscious mind from the past,

2

An increase in our patience, courage, and perseverance to undertake the challenges of life placed before us,

3

A detoxification of the negative energies associated with our present personality such as anger, jealousy, blame, resentments, and long held grievances.

4

Guidance to direct our lives into a meaningful direction filled with purpose, creativity, and satisfaction,

5

An increase in our sense of appreciation, magnanimity, and love that can become a consistent energy in our expression to others.

6

Certain concepts become more clear such as: a.) the oneness and interconnectedness of all things, b.) the importance of releasing the past through forgiveness and c.) that our true identity lies beyond the confines of our physical body.

Keep remembering that you are a sacred work in progress and that your gift of consciousness is the greatest power there is on the earth. However, few people know how to focus their consciousness in a truly powerful way. It might surprise you to find how much practice it requires to just maintain a focused state of awareness, without thinking, for even one minute. Try focusing your consciousness upon a finger or a toe until you can feel its effect in creating a sense of warmth or tingling. Then practice focusing on a place between your two eyes as you meditate.

The purpose of our life is to restore a connection with our core Self or soul in order to understand the true essence of life and how to integrate it into our personality. Meditation is a tool to this purpose, and becomes more powerful with its use. As such, it is an active skill that must be practiced. Meditation, to be progressively effective, must be accompanied by your strong intention to become a more loving being in your daily life regardless of the behavior of others around you. You are now beginning a journey that ends in the awareness of remembering who you are.

Part 1

Initially, you might expect to receive encouragement to reinforce your daily practice of meditation. All that is needed is faith, the willingness to listen, and a focused expectation that opens the door within oneself to receive. And you will receive what you need to hear at that moment in time. Each of the following selections is introduced by an unasked question.

How might I reach
You in meditation?

During meditation your mind wanders from thoughts of Me to one association after another until you are reminded that you are meditating and you pull yourself back to your original intention. This exercise should be practiced briefly throughout the day.

Your mind becomes so intrigued by the illusionary world that it travels quickly from one preoccupation to the next, and further and further from the awareness of who you are. You must practice to discipline the mind not to stray from the contemplation of Me and My relationship to you as your Creator.

All the world is like a movie screen upon which is projected your inner thoughts. If you can become aware of yourself as the viewer, detached from the consequences of the life and death struggle you are privy to watch, your experiences will be for learning, free from the anxiety and pain you now feel.

By turning your eyes inward toward Me, how much more wonderful is the joy you will experience than anything that might be projected upon the screen. So this is the lesson of all lessons: the turning of your eyes from creation to Creator.

How can I know when I have
made contact with You?

Today take your first real step into understanding the making of contact. Try to feel it as a glow within the head resting upon a radiant rod, the spine, and know that this is a beginning. Practice this as often as possible—and if this is not very often, then see that you make it more possible.

Remember that you attain this, not by mechanically following any ritualistic process, but mainly through the projection of all of your feelings and desires inward.

Once you have experienced the feeling of making contact, try to maintain it as long as possible. Then you will come to know what activities lead to strengthening, and what activities lead to weakening your tie with Me.

If you practice loving Me, then you will no longer fear Me. Remember, and know through practice, that love dispels all fears. Learn to see all of your fellow men as immortal beacons of My spirit, covered by an unreal outer facade of personality.

Why do I occasionally feel confused after an extended period of meditation?

The birth of awareness is often a blinding experience. And those accustomed to the dark will claim to see less in the light. Thus, a time of darkness often precedes the light. Persevere along the path, even when the way becomes temporarily obscure, for progress along a straight road can be continued in a heavy fog.

And sometimes the fog can make you more keenly aware of certain markings along the way which, in the light, you might tend to overlook.

There are many phases you must transit on the path of progress. But there is always provided a resting place before each cycle or level. Do not be uneasy when this occurs, but make use of the oasis to store the energy that will be needed for the next leg of the journey. And there is always an opportunity for the development of the will in overcoming impatience, discouragement, fatigue, and doubt.

The best use of your will is in constantly seeking to know who you are. Practice focusing upon Me. At first dimly or blurred, but then ever sharper and more distinct My reality will become as you practice.

What should I do when unhappy thoughts of the past bubble up when I meditate?

If you must relive the pains of your youth, relive also the joys—for in those days I was very close to your heart. You were able to feel Me then in the breath of the air, whether it was a summer breeze or the crisp gust from new-fallen snow.

You delighted in the new discovery of every living creature, whether it was on wing or creeping upon earth. The sun did then embrace you lovingly in its warmth, and the smell of grass, and the sound of busy activity of hidden insects all about filled you with an inner surge of life that now you so nostalgically seek to recover.

Remember Me! And let your rediscovery of Me be a balm to soothe all grief. Master the pain of the past with the joy of knowing I AM with you.

With so many books teaching how to meditate, how can I possibly know how to begin?

Persist daily along the present path as has been laid out for you. Digression into other areas only impedes your skillful mastery of one particular vehicle. Any method of seeking God, if approached with sincere desire and continued on a daily basis, will bring results beyond expectation.

For who can tell you how to reach your God? God, being everywhere present, may be reached by an infinite number of paths. But the paths must be narrow and straight, lest useful energy be diffused into idle sidetracks.

It is well to read of the ways chosen by the ancient holy men, but no mechanical repetition of another's design can carry you through the final stages. Choose one from many, or better still, seek your own. Desire for God is the only ingredient needed. Thus, no man should force upon another his own path, nor judge the way of any other.

God, why are You so elusive?

How easy it would be to find God if you saw Me beckoning to you from the distance. You could set out to reach Me down a sun-baked, dusty road until you either succeeded or else dropped from exhaustion.

How much harder it is to find My elusive face among a madhouse of mirrors and illusions and the distractions of comforts and sense pleasures that make the search appear either unnecessary or utterly hopeless!

But when the dreamer becomes sufficiently dissatisfied with the dream, awakening is not too far to follow. And when you learn to truly see, you will find that My face is in every mirror.

It is hard to believe that there is a personal
God who knows me and is willing to
communicate with me.

Continue patiently to seek Me, knowing that I am
never far away. Soon, very soon, My voice will become
more distinct. That will occur when you are truly ready
to accept the full responsibility of knowing My will in
all matters.

Keep open the channel for very personal messages,
accepting and trying what you receive before judging
the source. If your channel, through desire and prayer,
be open to Me, then you need never fear the influences
of other unwanted or uninvited sources.

Remember that all have this channel available to
them. So let whatever success you have be shared
primarily as an encouragement for others to initiate
their own conscious communications with Me. Let all
sharing be a sharing of Me. Help others to see Me in
whatever experience or pleasure you wish to share.

I am beginning to experience a sense of calmness when I meditate, but I can't find time to do it every day.

You say that you are too busy. Too busy to sleep? Too busy to eat or to exercise the body properly? Too busy to love? And what can you be so busily doing that takes precedence over all these? Especially since without these, the sources of all energy, you will not be keeping busy very long!

Take time; take time, My child, to replenish the spirit as well as the body. For you pray incessantly for God's love, yet take no time to sit still to receive it.

Seek constantly to experience God's love. But remember, to receive love, you must give it. Practice the giving of your love in little ways at every opportunity every day. This must be an important part of every activity—unselfish giving. Only then can you receive.

I still have difficulty shutting off all my busy thoughts and believing that there is really something else to hear.

The Universal Mind is always there to be tapped by those who would listen. Yet motives must be pure to make the link to the highest Source.

Notice how often the words of a speaker are distorted by the fears and ambitions and desires of the listener. Only a free mind can have a truly receptive ear.

And the concentration of the listener can only be maintained through respect for the source. Thus, in this way, far more than in any other, does one man pay his respect to another.

When the noise and the cares of the ego are stilled, how sweet, then, are the sounds that may be heard of life's symphony everywhere. And those who are easily bored are shut up within their own vanity, caring only for an audience for their own idle thoughts.

But if you must blind out all else, keep ever a receptive ear, and all of the secrets of life will one by one be opened up to you.

What am I really trying to discover through meditation?

Gratitude is most greatly experienced when that which was thought lost is found. A man may feel ungrateful at being offered a third leg or a third arm, but if that leg which he does have and which was thought to be hopelessly lame is restored to health, then will his gratitude toward the Master healer be uncontained.

Likewise, no bribe of a precious gem can equal the diamond hidden within, which when discovered, will overcome all need for competition and replace all jealousy with joy.

So hearken to the messengers God sends who would awaken you to your treasures within. But beware of the false prophet who would spew his own treasure before you in the hope of seeking adulation and praise.

For the truth which My messenger brings is this: Nothing shall be seen in him that is not already within your own self.

What should I focus upon
when I am meditating?

Be ever mindful of My presence within. When you pray, "God be with me," know that I am always with you and in you. It is you who must come to Me, to open your heart to My presence.

How best might this be done? Desire it! If your desire be strong enough and pure, the Kingdom might be yours in a single day. But how can a man travel with his mind idly searching the stars, while his feet remain rooted in the trivia of the earth? I am where the heart is.

Come to Me with an honest mind and the pure heart of an innocent child and with the desire of one who craves My love, and who, now homesick beyond all earthly consolation, seeks My presence.

Believe! Believe I am here within you. You have reached the limits of your progress unless your faith be now expanded to all parts of your being— your body, mind, and heart.

Sometimes good ideas come to me,
but then other thoughts discourage me from
acting upon them.

Notice how your second thoughts continually negate My presence and dissuade you from constructive action by false pessimism and doubt. If you would hear Me, listen! Then practice respecting that which your heart knows to be right before it is drowned in a flood of alternative considerations that lead only to mental paralysis and procrastination.

To hear and to heed My voice gives energy to the will and inspires further constructive action. To negate the inner voice leads to enervation, self recrimination, and guilt over that which is left undone and most probably never will be satisfactorily completed.

And why do you doubt your ability to hear My voice? It is always there, in every thought you think. But being given free will you are permitted to entertain alternative thoughts, such as those that might lead to immediate sense pleasure or idle diversion, until you learn gradually to choose with your heart and not with your mind.

So in every thought you have, find Me! Soon you will consciously begin the sifting process, choosing by your free will, the ego or Me. And then whichever you choose will be greatly strengthened within you, until the voice of the other is all but lost. Thus does man choose Heaven or Hell for himself. Judge, then, your own present state of purity by how clear you maintain your channel to Me.

Self-Pride Closes the Ears to Learning

Continue in your pursuit of greater awareness, and this will lead inevitably to greater humility. And with the gradual development of humility you will dare to be closer to Me. With sincerity and humility you can stand in the presence of the Christ without trembling. As the Master taught, strive to be as a little child in your acceptance, awareness, and appreciation of all things, looking enthusiastically toward the next experience.

But man, as he ages and learns a few things, falls into vanity and self-pride. Then he believes that he knows it all and stubbornly refuses to listen. He grows competitive with other similarly self-deceived men, and because he is able to prove them wrong, becomes more convinced of his own self-righteousness. To maintain this illusionary status, he develops insincerity and deceit. But within himself his spirit knows the error of his ways and would tremble mightily if faced with the presence of the Undeceived.

No man can ever prove a humble man wrong since he never tries to be right, but only just. From his lips would never pass a deceitful word, for knowing the extent of his own ignorance, he would never seek to increase it in another.

But knowing that God puts wisdom even in the mouth of babes, he will ever listen with a careful ear to all who speak, lest he miss a precious message from his Lord.

It is well that you pray for humility, for this is the key that opens the Gate, the virtue that leads to all others.

Part 2

Almost coincident with the initial excitement and the belief that contact is possible, we tend to superimpose the barrier of self consciousness and feelings of unworthiness that pushes God once more into the distance. Then we begin to invalidate His presence. We fall into self-doubt and discouragement and feel the need for reassurance. Somehow, answers come to our questions even before we know enough to ask them.

I have been meditating for some time. How
long will it take before I become more aware
and intuitive?

You are just beginning to listen. The wisdom of
all the ancients is yours who are willing to hear it. Be
not dismayed by slow progress. Neither compare your
development with others, for all are judged by an
invisible measurement, peculiar to the individual. Each
has his work to do and is given the help necessary to
accomplish the task.

And how can a man with the gift of prophesy be
compared to a man with a gift of tongues, or to a
man who has neither gift, yet dwells in inner peace in
God's love? Each is given according to his needs and
the dictates of his circumstances.

I am still overwhelmed by all my responsibilities, and I don't know how to bring the calmness of meditation into my daily life.

Do not becone frustrated by the lack of obvious signs of progress. You can only guess at the ways in which progress might be measured. No man, no matter how unworthy he deems himself, if he ardently and faithfully seeks Me, cannot help but find himself eventually in My presence.

As you go through this period of readjustment of your values, you will naturally become somewhat discouraged by your expenditure of energy into unrewarding channels. The only solution is to stop and make an abrupt change in your course now.

Decide how best you might use your time, and let not external pressures prevail upon you. Be humble in the heaping of your tasks. No man can function at the extreme limits of his capabilities for days and weeks unending. In small ways, in small things conscientiously accomplished, do you reach your goal.

Seek enjoyment in the activities of each hour and with pleasure anticipate the next. Do not let your daily work become a drudgery which depletes your life energy. Decide what must be done this day and the time that will be allotted to it, and then let your pleasure be in the doing of it.

Let your heart dance with joy, My child, for only then can your blood assimilate the breath of life. Learn the secret of bringing joy to every task you perform. In surrendering in small ways, in the doing of small things, is the barrier of stubbornness, rebellion, and resistance broken.

Remember that "overwhelmed" is a state of mind perpetuated by inner struggle. But place yourself in the rhythm of doing one small thing well at a time, and all that you could hope for will soon be done. Offer each task to Me and together we will work as one.

Be ever conscious of your need to attune and reattune constantly to My pattern, Law, or Will (as you wish) lest you stray too far and be lost to Me. The quality of your love is a measure of your attunement to Me.

I am still struggling to find time to meditate
on a daily basis. I wonder if You are really
interested in the details of my daily life.

You are still filled with many doubts as to the
closeness and reality of My presence, but with the
passing of each day your watchful eyes will become
more and more believing. Pray more frequently when
faith grows dim and at frequent intervals during every
day, for prayer is your link to Me—the affirmation of
your desire to make contact with Me.

Try to believe that I am constantly returning your
communications and soon, very soon, you will know
My presence within. Do not expect to hear My voice
as strange, or distinctly within or without, but rather
as the generative force beyond and behind your own
thoughts.

Believe in My Love until you feel it. See the
importance to your own development in your daily
tasks; yet never become so preoccupied with doing,
that you lose the thread to understanding the true
Source and Meaning of all things.

Strength grows through the constant practice of
attuning to Me. And let not overconfidence and
carelessness carry you so far away from the Source of
the sound that you forget the beat to which you must
attune.

Today, I gave my little daughter a new toy to play with because I wanted to meditate and did not want to be distracted by her. But she pushed it away and held out her little arms to me saying, "I want you-u-u. I want to be with you-u-u." and it cut my heart so that I had to embrace her.

Then I tried this approach in my meditation, and to the extent that I could duplicate her innocence and sincerity, God could not resist it either.

As Jesus said "Unless you become as an innocent child you shall not enter into the kingdom of heaven." Innocence is the state of total honesty and total acceptance. With this comes purity of heart and a reestablishment of one's bond with God. The pure in heart are always appreciative, never selfish, and are filled with loving.

What about those days when I have too
much to do and feel too exhausted and
overwhelmed to meditate?

Learn to overcome weariness, my child, by a constant act of will that directs all activity toward ultimate good. Accept, first, your weariness without compounding your problems by seeking comfort or satiation where it is not to be found. Rather, in your weariness, do what must be done without self-pity or temptations toward indulgence. For everything has its season and its cycle, and God's work must continue throughout.

Be not dismayed by discouraging results or uncomfortable comparisons. Remember, each person travels along their own unique path to spiritual development, and resistances and obstacles are always placed before you to test the will.

Learn the secret of the heart which must work constantly to maintain life, yet rests between every beat. Thus, in every activity there is the opportunity to exercise one faculty while resting another.

Why do I still feel so much tension?.

Tension comes from trying, and not from doing. It grows out of expectations, both good and bad, but never from acceptance. Tension comes from dissatisfaction with the image you present, never from the humble belief that you are enough if your heart be right. Tension arises from your judgments of your fellowman, which are then turned upon yourself.

Tensions arise from neglect of the body which cannot be denied its rest, its exercise, and its proper nourishment. Tensions arise from the guilt of your errors and the regrets of the past when nothing is being done to correct the future. Tension arises from the struggle within, whether to follow the head or the heart and when to know the difference. Tension arises out of the resistance to temptations to which you have already given your assent.

My child, avoid the needless expense of tension by surrendering it to Me. Once your decision is made to do this without ambivalence, so that no further decisions need be made, you will marvel at how quickly tensions will cease.

Do not struggle within, when all that is needed is a mutual attunement to the same song of life. Let your heart provide the beat and your feet take up the dance and observe how all the elements fall quickly into step.

God, I have so many things that I
would like to do, but I can never find
the time to do them.

Make a beginning. Nothing is ever accomplished without a beginning. Put yourself in the frame of mind necessary to make a beginning, caring not at the moment about the end result. Your mind cannot contain the finished product which you feel you need before you begin. Even a poor beginning is better than none. But procrastination is the bane of the world, and the sins of omission are those which will bring about the gnashing of teeth.

Ponder on this thought awhile: How well are you able to initiate that which you have an initial impulse to do? In the answer to this lies the difference between the man who leaves his mark upon the world and he who suffers the misery of a wasted life. Let not a second impulse overcome the first, but reinforce it by returning again and again to it, that initial, fleeting impulse to action given to you. Strive to discipline your life to become a smooth and continuous pattern of completed actions as they are given by Me to you to perform. Only then can total attunement be made with the one silver thread which unites us all.

Pray first for the proper attitude and, then, pray for My further help and inspiration.

How do I get over becoming discouraged by my weaknesses?

Do not be discouraged or dismayed by the recognition of your many weaknesses and limitations, for all that you admire in self makes it only the more difficult to surrender to Me. Strive constantly to free your heart, which is ever pure, knowing that I desire no other offering from you. So long as you are aware of the battle within, you will ultimately win.

Complacency is your greatest enemy and despair its ultimate tool. In all that you do, consider its impact upon your own spiritual development. Strive against all temptations which lead to judging yourself unkindly.

It is the small things each man encounters moment by moment and day by day that will either destroy him or lead him to the kingdom. And no other man or circumstance of events external to you can block your progress, once your heart is set upon the spiritual path. All suffering then becomes a boon and all unkindness, an opportunity to exercise your faith.

I have made such a mess of my life
that I don't know whether it's possible
to put it together now.

Never be dismayed, My child. Know that all error is merely the taking of a path leading in a direction away from the light of God. And once you have discovered your error, what is to prevent you from turning about to return along the path to your Father's home? Do not be like the man who, setting out in his new car upon a long journey, becomes lost in a maze of crossroads and byways, and after a considerable way, consults his map and finds that he has been heading in the wrong direction; but now, out of guilt and self-reproach, refuses to change his direction.

Judge not yourself by the garments you wear. Neither continue to conduct your life to conform your actions and your thoughts to the false image of your present personality. By so doing, you only augment its reality in your mind. See yourself literally as Jesus, or Buddha, or Yogananda, if you choose, knowing that you are what you think, and digest, and produce through your actions.

Dare to be that which you most admire in the hardiest of men. Be not discouraged by the enormity of the task. With the proper faith and conviction, it might be accomplished within a single day. And why do you doubt this, inasmuch as all that is required is refusing to see what is unreal and acknowledging that which *is*.

How do I handle my feelings when my friends
treat me with a superior attitude because
they have a better house, car, or income?

Strive always toward this end: that you be worthy
unto yourself. Man expends much energy in the
justifying of self through the accumulation of material
possessions or even by long hours of work. But can
your worth be measured by the size of your house or
rich monthly income?

You, who deem yourself of so little value, do you
feel, through an expensive house or car, you are worth
more? Let each be judged on its own system. How
can an immortal soul be totaled up with mortal
trinkets? No, this can never be. Yet men are ever
trapped in the folly of this reasoning. Rather strive
toward the perfection of self.

What the soul learns in attuning to the harmony
of God can never be taken away from it. Judge
yourself, separate from all others and all material things.

Each day is one more struggle with the same old problems. I'm not even sure that my petty problems deserve Your attention.

Your worthiness to Me is not measured by your motives and desires nor by the seemingly trivial tasks that you perform. My love for you is as complete as if you were alone in creation. Such is the nature of My love, infinite at every point it falls.

Ask not that I come to you, but that your consciousness be open to Me. Know that all your thoughts are Mine, and learn to trace them back to the ultimate Source.

Learn first to calm and still the mind, so accustomed is it to following the course of thought in a dozen different directions at once.

Let My gift to you today be this thought: Behind the frenzy and the fury, I AM. Contemplation upon this idea will bring you unexpected results. See every day as having a special significance of its own. Strive to expand each into a mini-life of its own. Thus we may celebrate a new birthday each hour.

There is so much chaos and conflict at
work that no one seems to appreciate how
much I offer? Is it all worth it!

Let not the storm outside distract or prevent the attunement within. Notice how you have been buffeted to and fro by your too high regard for the opinions of others. It is well to listen and to consider all sides before undertaking any activity of potential serious import, but let this not be an impediment to the knowing of your own heart within.

Preparation begins with prayer, proceeds through your efforts to attune your heart, and flows with the industrious completion of each task as it is placed before you.

If you desire to give to others, then practice giving to others. Give to every form of life, no matter how high or low you may esteem it, until the flow of your giving becomes a natural process without judgment or reservations.

Remember, you experience only that which is created within. So look within for the weakness that has made you vulnerable to abuse. Then give your love so freely that those who are unable to accept it will be forced to look within themselves for the source of their disharmony.

I can't believe that the consciousness
that runs the universe loves me.

Your Father's love is always total, unequivocal, and without reservation for all things which He has created. And how could it be otherwise? For being pure, His thoughts are pure, and all that He conceives and creates comes forth out of pure love. Love that is pure cannot be earned, increased, or changed in any way.

And all of life's experiences are but to teach you this: all you need ever do is to accept. Even when you cannot comprehend, you must accept. The man who cannot accept and who hates himself is always dangerous to others, while the man who truly accepts himself becomes a font of love to others.

Look again at all of God's creations and see the beauty in them. Why should it be different for you? Does not the deer love her doe and the bear fondle her cubs with love?

But man in his selfishness and ego-striving, tends to belittle his own offspring and thus teaches them to shun themselves. Let your greater wisdom overcome your fears and doubts, and learn from the lessons which God places before you. The heart must lead the brain, for love is to be experienced and cannot ever be totally comprehended.

It is difficult to really know that all I experience
is under Your direction and nothing is
disturbed unnecessarily.

Do not be overwhelmed by the fact of My
omnipresence. Your consciousness may attune to
Mine, and then every experience becomes a shared joy.
But you have a choice as to what path your
consciousness will follow—the path of the ego, which
places you in competition with others, the path of the
lower self which leads to dissipation of energy through
self-indulgence, or the path to Me which gives you life
through losing self.

The selfish individual, who has no time for others,
cannot believe or comprehend the personal nature of
My caring. Your happiness in Me is My joy, and your
sorrow in the ways of the world touches My heart with
compassion. Believe in Me, and the superficiality and
illusion of all else will vanish.

If your faith is so weak, then behave as though I
am there until your fears are tempered and you dare
to open your eyes to Me. But can you give up the
way of the ego and the path of self-indulgence in order
to follow Me? All that is needed is desire, and this
must surely come out of the lessons of life that teach
so clearly the pain and futility of another way.

I am uplifted by some of the thoughts that come to me in meditation, but when I try to share these with my friends, they often make light of them.

Free yourself from the past, the dependence upon others to determine your path, the entanglements of competition, and the dead-end pursuit of self-justification. The old ways lead to entanglement and confusion at the expense of spiritual energy better used for more productive purposes.

Even when a man has found the right Path, for a time he often insists upon strewing it with snares from his old ways, or else continues to carry upon his back the useless possessions of the past.

Rather, let your faith grow as a seed within your heart, nourished by a secret love, until that day when, in full bloom, the precious flower may be displayed before all the world. Show not your new-found treasures to fools, lest a thief break in and steal them all away. Remember, a wise man does not try to convert a fool, but neither would he ever provoke one needlessly. Live what you learn, and work only for those things which can never be stolen from you.

For the past few days I haven't
had time to meditate or even
think about God.

Whether you feel My presence or not, yet believe that I am always there, intimately involved with your every experience, no matter how slight. In fact, it is your attention, your involvement, your full appreciation of each experience that is lacking and not Mine. Your preoccupation with yesterday and your anticipation of tomorrow prevents you from being fully with Me now.

Learn to put everything into My hands. What can you of yourself accomplish? If you do faithfully what is given at this moment, tomorrow will be more than adequately handled.

Within each man is given a conscience as to what might be the best use of his energies at any time. Ask yourself: What should I really be doing now? And the answer, if you will face it, will come. And never let your time become so expensive that you cannot afford to give a few moments to God.

When I try to meditate, thoughts from the past come up. I think about things I should have done differently.

Memories of the past direct the actions of today. You must view all memories as dream sequences, freeing yourself from their awful entanglements. You cannot attain God while yet there are battles to be fought on earth. Your real battle is an internal one, to stop fighting! Forgive your enemies, embrace unrestrainedly your loved ones, and rejoice in the release of all hostilities and in the enjoyment of peace. Do not be hesitant or afraid to envision a pleasurable future for yourself and your family and your friends.

Buttressing yourself against evil by its constant anticipation only tends to create that which is feared. Certainly, once you have created and fixed the feared possibility in your mind, then you have already begun to suffer the consequences of its existence. For one thing, it greatly handicaps you from creating pleasurable alternatives. This does not mean that you should remain naive to real dangers, but why waste your creative energies in fighting imaginary battles while more constructive work is left undone.

Let today be a beginning. Practice cheerful optimism, which permits you to enjoy the things you now have, and pray for assistance in the difficult or tiresome tasks that need to be done. You must first make the effort, and then assistance will come that will suddenly make the task appear easy!

I have been doing a lot of praying about my family situation and I wonder if this helps and whether my prayers are doing any good.

It is well that you pray for help, for pride in man often prevents his reaching out to sources beyond his comprehension for what is needed to succeed.

Vain man! Asleep in ignorance as he is, yet obsessed with delusions of his own capabilities. Pride walks alone. Yet who does he expect will commend him for this! Seeing himself as the doer he is crippled with the guilt of his failures and tormented by the anxieties of indecision.

As you would help another, first you must receive help. Ask only for that which you would gladly give to another. There is joy in My giving just as there will be in your receiving. Learn to ask. God's supply of gifts for those who ask is inexhaustible. Learn to ask for your own development and the development of humility.

Through constant prayer all wrongs are righted, all pains are soothed, all fears dissolved. Practice constantly your communication with Me, and slowly, like the timid deer who gradually accepts a morsel from the outstretched hand of his keeper, so your apprehensions, doubts, and fears of Me will shortly vanish.

How do I approach my chores with the belief that even the simplest tasks have significance on a higher level?

Believe! As you believe, so it is. But man only believes what he desires to believe, and so it is well that you are discovering that there is no solace from your grief, no balm for your pain, and no joy in your walk through the world without Me. Desire to believe and patiently remove all barriers, all lies, all temptations that weaken your faith and your desire to know Me.

The heart knows, and it must be opened before I can come to you. Give your heart a chance. Think less with your head and feel more with your heart. And be open to seeing things in a different way than you have seen them before.

I am here, beside you, within you, all around you, and yet you see Me not. This is not of My doing or desire, but your own. Know that this part is in your hands and everything else is in Mine. Practice leading with your heart and, soon, all that you do will be reawakened to life anew.

What is the primary attitude that I must hold to fully accept Your Presence?

Sincerity! Seek to direct your mind with total sincerity in every activity you choose. Seek never for selfish gain, but rather for that which will lead to greater understanding and wisdom.

Never confuse humility with unworthiness, for what can you do to be worthy of Me, but to desire Me? What can you ever give, but acceptance of Me?

So how might you serve Me? Surrender yourself totally to My will. Know only that you can never know Me. See yourself as totally incapable of accomplishing a single thing by yourself. Desist in your constant resistance to me, and let Me be the guide of your every thought and activity. Everything I have is yours to share.

Thus, curb your attitudes of impatience, anger, apprehension and pride. Seek to maintain constantly the happy predisposition of an innocent child—accepting, open, expectant, and grateful.

Do not count your worldly gifts as spiritual attainment. You yearn to "see," and divine, and speak in tongues, yet can you see what a detriment such gifts would be to your greater development?

All that you must know will be given at the proper time. Strive, instead, for an attitude of sincerity, acceptance, and humility. Let Me do the rest. Do not be afraid. I accept all your burdens gladly. How better might you come to know My Love?

Remember that nothing that you or anyone else does has any real meaning other than the way that you do it. Do everything as if your life depended upon it, without shirking your responsibilities and placing them upon others.

Maintain a cheerful, accepting, and uncomplaining attitude, remembering that nothing that lives is less or more important than you. All are equally loved in God's eyes, and all have a place in His plan. Rather, be grateful for your growing awareness, like a flowering plant in the morning sun.

Part 3

The next major step to spiritual development consists in the cultivation of right attitude that will eventually lead to maturity, responsibility, sincerity, humility, and purity of heart. The nature and importance of these virtues must now be understood. The following pages provide enlightening thoughts on these subjects while the fact of God's constant presence is continually reinforced.

On Purity of Heart

How do you think you will be judged when you come face to face with your Master, as indeed one day you will? Not by the dirt of labor under your fingernails, or the learning you have accumulated in your mind and brain, or by the health or cleanliness of your physical body, but by the purity of your heart: whether it be kind, giving, and unselfish and, above all, totally open in innocent receptivity to God's love.

See therefore that all your present efforts are directed toward the place of greatest reward. For of what value is the gift of immortality if the desires of your heart be fixed upon mortal things. And of what avail is your lonely searching for love when your heart is closed to God's love which is everywhere abundant in inconceivable intensity about you.

But the joy of receiving leads to the joy of giving. The heart that is cloaked in selfishness cannot be receptive to the Source of Love, and receiving nothing, has nothing to give.

On Humility

True humility is the seeking of My answer without thought of how it might appeal to you or to another. But pride constantly censors, distorts, and re-edits all truth to its own purposes.

True humility detaches one from the arena of competition, knowing that the source of all his wisdom and strength comes from God who favors no one.

True humility never presupposes, is not committed to results or outcomes, and strives constantly to change only himself.

True humility never judges, never punishes, never "kids" or jokes, never embarrasses, never defeats, never fights, never predicts, never impresses, and never forgets the needs of others.

Humility opens up what pride buries and conceals. Humility soothes where pride incites. Humility is silent where pride speaks, it listens and learns where pride spews his knowledge, it gives where pride takes, it compliments where pride criticizes, and helps when pride fights.

Only in total humility is man able to surrender to Me. For all of his vanity and selfishness and pride keeps him tightly encased within a shell of his own making. But when humility softens the heart to receive God's love, it grows and bursts its confining walls.

Then like a seed bursting from its pod, or a butterfly from its cocoon, or a baby from its mother's womb, it welcomes its glorious rebirth into an entirely new existence.

On Overcome Resistance to Praying

No one by his or her own efforts has ever found peace. Without a connection to your Source you cannot know who you are, what you want, or what is your purpose. How can you see anything but problems when you decide blindly what you must accomplish? And in your weariness you blame others for not providing the assistance and support you need. Thus you join them in your self-dissatisfaction and guilt.

Everything that you have placed within your own mind has no real meaning. Only the Holy Spirit can tell you who you are and of your relationship to God. Only the Holy Spirit can tell you your importance and how much you are loved. Only then can you be a totally loving being. Only then will your problems evaporate, one by one, like miracles.

Pray often for wisdom and God's graces. Know that you are but a tiny twig upon the tree of life and need help and nourishment from the tree to flourish and grow. Never hesitate to ask for help.

The branch cannot grow leaves of its own accord but must draw from the life-sap of the main trunk in order to share in the glory of the tree.

On Controling Your Tongue
Through Right Thinking

When a man sequesters angry, defiant, critical, or unclean thoughts of any kind, they soon will defile him through his speech. The solution, then, is not to hold thy tongue (though it be well that you recognize the occasions when your tongue would best be held) but rather to maintain at all times right thinking. Nurture within, only those thoughts that you wish to blossom within your heart and, when expressed, will make a sweet sound upon the ear of God. Only then will He accept you into His holiest places.

But be not dismayed when many times daily, your Ego challenges you with flashes of unworthy thoughts. See that you summarily dismiss each one, lingering not to taste its flavor before you send it on, lest enough such savored thoughts will make an unclean meal that festers within your innermost parts and reproduces more of its own kind.

Yet, how quickly might consistent right thinking raise a man from his earthly woes!

On The Attitude of Respect

As with the giving of love and the expression of all virtues, so only by the giving of respect to others can one truly feel respect for himself.

So much meaning might be found in that one word. It means the acknowledgment and consideration of the right of others to a full life and an equal sharing of all of God's gifts. It means a recognition of the fact of God's indwelling presence in every form of life. It implies a caring for the needs of others and a concern for their well-being, equal to that of oneself. It means a willingness to listen or, more, a desire to receive the expressions of life and awareness given by God uniquely to every being and creature form. It means recognizing the rightness and importance of another's existence as equal to your own. It means a willingness to give, up to the point of stifling the patterns within self of selfishness that might prevent one from sharing all. It means allowing the other to maintain the center of the stage while you stand aside in true humility. It entails the recognition and the appreciation of the true value of another.

Respect means accepting with empathy and compassion the life role and behavior of another, while refraining from all criticism and harsh judgments. It means being able to say within your heart, "Thank you for being there. Thank you for being you".

On Maturity

Maturity is a state of mind that gives a special quality to all action.

It is an attitude and a feeling of sober reverence and respect for whatever circumstances one finds himself experiencing, and an openness to the many lessons at many levels being taught by every situation of life.

It is knowing that ultimately nothing whatsoever really matters save that God is. It is acting in the constant conscious awareness of the death of the body.

It is a striving for fulfillment in accordance with the deeper spiritual conscience within, undaunted by the urges and cravings of the lower self.

It means getting out of self by focusing one's energies toward empathy and compassion for others.

To accept that you understand nothing allows you to see everything, and to encapsulate time into an infinite string of "nows", each a complete vignette, with an experience and a lesson of its own, mindful of nothing preceding, contemplating nothing succeeding, hearing only the inner voice of the Master.

To be mature is to be as a lamb, to see as a child, and yet to have perfect control over one's thoughts and actions. It means never to be dissuaded by the judgments of others, but to hold sole responsibility for one's actions, caring never for consequences when one follows his heart.

The mature man is constantly judging his motives and setting them straight, guided never by fear or vanity or hope of worldly gain, but by the inner calling of the heart that would return him once more to his father All.

The Man of God Is Not a Revolutionary

The revolutionary is brave because he is resigned to his death, whereas the man of God is brave because he knows that there is no death. The strength of the revolutionary comes from his anger which he projects upon others, and he uses the tools of the ego to satisfy his needs. His acts are ego-driven and buttressed by an uncommon sense of self-righteousness. He follows a master plan carefully conceived out of vanity and of ignorance to the true underlying evolution of all things. He sees himself as having the power to change the future course of events in accordance with his own vain thinking, and seeks the adulation of future generations for his efforts. He surrounds himself with admirers so that he becomes so entangled in his folly that there is little hope for the light of truth to enter.

The man of God seeks no ends for himself, nor presupposes a better plan for man's salvation than that which is. He knows that the true enemy is within, and displacing faith from himself to God, takes strength to oppose the compelling of the false ego. When a man has found his own will, he loses all desire to compel the obedience of the wills of others. The man of God shows great courage in living his own life according to his deepest ideals, even when deemed eccentric by those about him, and is silenced only by wisdom and never by fear. The man of God listens to everyone alike, but harkens only to the voice that comes from within the heart.

On Loneliness and Depression

Often when a person has lost a loved one, for whatever reason, they undergo a long period of sadness and grief and may even lose their desire to live. Whenever you lose the desire to live it is because you have ceased to allow the feeling of love to flow through you. Begin to pray for others and begin to send them your love, and you will begin to know yourself as the ultimate source of love.

Your inner Self is always joyful. It is only the ego-self that suffers loss and feels despair. However the saddest and most depressing moments of your life can become a window to making a stronger contact with Me. Use such times in this way and eventually there will come a feeling of peace.

Be thankful for every moment of your life. Only then will your heart-strings be stirred to the vibration of love that will free you. Be joyful for My presence in everything and everywhere. And as the ever-changing scene brings before you new and different experiences, know that it is I, presenting Myself to you in different ways and forms for the purpose that you might come to know Me. I Am everywhere and in everything. Why then should you ever experience loneliness?

On Seeking God's Love

When all of your motives are for the seeking of God's love, then you may demand of God, as His child, to show you His face. Know the anguish of losing Him and the comparative trivial worth of anything else you might have to lose.

Do not be reconciled by anything less than the vivid image and warmth of That presence, and God will not deny you anymore. Seek God as with the longing for a lost love, or as Rachael crying in grief for her lost children. Then will God be moved to pity and raise you up into His heart.

Take care that in periods of your resting you seek not the consolation of worldly pleasures, forgetting the deeper yearning of your soul. Be discontent with all you possess, as long as you cannot see the face of God upon it. Look for the signs of Love and Presence everywhere and in everything you experience. As God becomes more real, so too will His love, for God's reality is Love.

See God's expression in every child and living thing and make your overtures of love to them as you would directly to God. Sow love to God everywhere until the mask is removed and Divine Presence is revealed. But only the purest and the most intense desire will ever persuade God to allow this to be opened to you.

On the Importance of Surrendering

Surrendering means giving up, on every level, your servitude to the ego and to attune all thinking, motives, and actions to My guiding direction.

You are still struggling needlessly against Me. In all that you do with the expectation of future gain or future accomplishment, great expenditures of energy are required, with often disappointing results. As long as your thoughts are in the future, you can never find happiness in The Now. Your sharing with Me must be *Now!*

All judgments you make regarding the future must necessarily come into conflict with Me, for no one can know My plan unless I reveal it to him. Even then, it can never be totally understood in all its purposes and implications. See Me as viewing you through loving eyes, every moment. Surrender your thinking and your actions to Me.

Believe first in your need for God's love until your desire grows and leads you there. Believe in My presence; pray for faith; listen with eagerness to My words and then believe!

Read these words often and pray for a deeper understanding of them.

On Learning the Lesson of Surrender

Practice focusing your inner eye upon an awareness that supersedes all your thoughts until you arrive at the realm of Presence and the realization that you are not alone. Dare to open your mind to the highest conception of your own being imaginable. Dare to believe that you are created of the same essence as the saints and that all consciousness is one, belonging ultimately to God

Then, learn the lesson of surrender. Do not hold your thoughts to yourself, nor accept those as your own that offend you. Learn, by practice, to stand aside and watch the process of thought within until you can sift and discard as suits your will. All thought, all consciousness, all being, all activity and energy force comes from God, without which the world, as you know it, would vanish. All is sustained in His thoughts as an expression of His being. Yet, you are given free will to entertain whatever thoughts that you choose. Then you suffer unnecessary pain and anxiety by your refusal to surrender to Him while allowing your own unwanted thoughts to control you. Your fear to surrender arises out of your doubt of His caring and His love for you.

The thoughts of God are inconceivable to man, and His plan more glorious than mortal mind can comprehend. And each person, if he knew his own place in God's plan, would be filled with uncontained joy. Then all your jealousy would vanish and be replaced by love for all those who participate and share with you in the unfolding of life's drama.

On Overcoming Apprehensions About the Future

Be always assured that those who consider God beyond all else need to fear nothing else. Immurse yourself in the thought, "Thy will be done," and at every crossroad of your life you will know the peace that comes from total acceptance. Neither stars, nor planets, not all of the forces of evil can prevail upon you in any way when your eyes and heart are set upon God. Know that the trials and tribulations you experience are a necessary part of your development. Accept all that comes graciously. Instead of snares, see them in the light of learning experiences.

Believe in the closeness of God's presence. Seek ever to feel that presence, and you will not be disappointed. The fruit you seek rests already in your palm, yet so much work needs still be done before you totally acknowledge and are willing to clasp your fingers to it.

But be not dismayed. Rather, be ever light in your heart, knowing that situations bringing discouragements are still steps forward. Go without fear. Follow the dictates of the heart, and be not concerned for results. Progress is achieved in the state of your heart, and never by the judgments of others upon you. Dismiss your fears. Leave them to rest with God.

Part 4

All life experiences present opportunities for growth, but none of these are as important as our relationships with our daily acquaintances and our immediate family. Guidance is given here for the proper conduction of our daily activities and interactions with our fellow-man. By these actions we might measure our level of spiritual growth.

Selfishness is the First
Barrier to Overcome.

Selfishness was born the day that man saw himself as an entity separate unto himself from others. Then his concerns were for the survival of this self beyond all other concerns.

And sometimes the interests of the self become more important than the body of the self, and there follows martyrdom for a cause. But so long as self is served or justified by any action, then this, too, is selfishness.

There is only one cause worth dying for, and that is the Oneness of Man and the reality of his relationship to his Maker. For only by the recognition and knowing of this can man be freed from selfishness. Only then can all of his motives and purposes serve the eternal and universal good. In dealing with himself in others, man lost himself. In finding himself in others, man may become free.

Spiritual Growth Includes Caring
for Self and Family

In the process of growth man must play many roles, perform many functions, and experience every possible relationship with his fellow man. And those that appear gifted are not greater than those who are served. For man's yardstick is not God's, who sees everyone of equal worth.

Thus, refrain from exalting yourself when placed in a position of authority or power. But see the greater perspective of your first duty to self and to family. Nothing that you do is more important than this.

Ask yourself then: What might best be served at this time for my own greater spiritual development? And family is always the first priority. How often this question is overlooked in man's supposed unselfish dedication to his work and in service to others? And how often behind the veil of dedication and service does one find the twin devils of vanity and pride?

Never feel pressed into God's service to the neglect of family or self. For God has abundance of time and is not impatient for the unfolding of His plan. All ideas come from God and are meant to be shared unselfishly. And man is given a little knowledge to see whether he can be trusted with more. But there is no holding back from the man who is truly humble.

Thus, guard your motives and pray that they be pure, and assess daily God's gifts and your proper use of them. When your motives are pure, all help is there; but that done out of vanity or pride will exact a heavy price.

How to Avoid Needless Suffering

Learn in all of your daily activities to gradually change the flow from oneself to others. Selfish thought, which is an indwelling preoccupation with self only, creates a prison wall that becomes ever more impervious to the love and blessings of God. In cutting yourself off from God, you expose yourself to terrible needless suffering.

God never meant for you to suffer. Create within your own mind only those thoughts and attitudes that you would wish to live with for all eternity, for the Kingdom is within and you are the creator of it.

Those thought and ideals that lead to eternal bliss and oneness with the All-knowing are being constantly given by the still Voice within, being always available for those who will listen. But you have been given free will to take and to choose as you please.

All too often, man harkens to the dictates of the false ego and brings evil upon himself, or he succumbs to the urges of the lower self and manages to entrap himself in selfishness and procrastination which weakens the power of the will.

Surround yourself frequently with the spiritual-minded, and read frequently the words of Holy Scripture and of wise sages of the past. The mind thus attuned to hearing the Good Word, like the gourmet accustomed to fine wines, will quickly identify and discard all that is inferior.

Your Greatest Challenge is
Within Your Own Home

You must break the bonds that hold you to the past and that now make you see yourself and others in an unreal light. The opportunity comes within your own home. Be responsible for the happiness of every member of your family, rather than seek cause to complain about their inability to satisfy your own needs. Search within for the cause of all discord. Be the one to make the first concession, the necessary adjustment, the important decision, the soothing remark and the supportive compliment.

Blind yourself not to your children's deeper emotional needs, but rather become a model for the open and spontaneous expression of feeling. Strive always to be happy, to elevate your attitude and outlook to the joyful and optimistic, and raise the mood of those about you by your frequent expressions of appreciation and enjoyment.

You are the builder of the home, and if the structure crumbles, who will you have to blame? But the home without reflects the state of the temple within, and no man can turn his eyes from one with the excuse of building the other.

Know yourself, then, by what is reflected in the eyes of your most intimate family. Nowhere is your influence so important or your opportunity for development so great.

Kindness is God Working Through You

Notice how that which you wish for another becomes your own, and how praying for a friend opens your heart to Me. Let this, then, be a measure of your spiritual growth, how openly, sincerely, and often your thoughts and prayers are for others. For through you, and not in you, will I make My presence known.

Let your joy be in the giving of Me to others and then will you be filled with an abundance of My presence. Make a beginning, no matter how awkward, to do that which you know will please Me until it becomes natural, a habit, and part of your own image.

Prepare yourself for any encounter with your fellow man, colleague, friend, competitor or opponent, by seeing first the beauty that is in them. God alone reserves the right to chastise His own children. Yet, when you allow Him to speak through you to set them aright, then He is well pleased. And you will find that no one can resist a humble man who is sincere in his convictions.

But in gathering in My lost sheep, you must be careful not to drag them back with a tight grip upon their throat. For each must of his own accord be guided to the Light of reason.

Seek to Know Your
True Responsibilities

Do not be disquieted by the complexities of your life. If you are overwhelmed, it is only because you have taken tasks upon yourself that should be of no concern to you while neglecting that which is your true responsibility.

If you would but resign yourself completely to the fact that all is in My hands, and cease to wrestle with Me for control, then you would find energies enough to focus upon your own very small, but nonetheless important part I ask you to play.

Take one step at a time and do well that which occurs to you to do. And how often are your inspired ideas or intentions put aside by the intrusion of your indolent reasoning mind?

Begin today to practice one step at a time.

Communication Begins With Listening

Be not concerned with selling yourself, rather than speaking the truth. Know that a good listener is far more often in the position of making a powerful impact upon another than the avid speaker. For when a man's mouth is forced closed, often too are his ears.

But when you allow him the chance to speak, his ears open up to hear himself talk, and then can you best attune to his level of thinking and offer a comment that will strike deep and which he cannot avoid considering without much thought.

Do not be concerned about your impact upon others. The bonds between men are forged in heaven, and no effort of wit is needed to bind you closer to those with whom you feel an affinity.

No meeting among men comes about by accident. Neither must you always know the full import of every chance encounter, but be content to let the parts play themselves out as they will.

Have more concern for the truth, and less for show. Strive to become a man of few words, well chosen, but with an open mind, willing to listen to all.

No one speaks to you in vain. But everyone you meet has some merit worthy of your attention.

Judgment is a Barrier to Learning

Try to see the weaknesses in self, instead of denouncing the faults of others. For the defects which you denounce in others are given to you as a mirror by which you might better examine yourself.

Remember that your heart can receive or accept only that which you are willing to give. Thus, when you bolster another with honest affection, your heart opens up to receive affection from another. And when you give harsh judgments or withhold praise, notice that you also complain that that is all you receive from others.

In all of your social interactions, seek an opportunity to give to others that which you need. This is a simple rule, yet men fail to see its benefits when they are too mindful of receiving while in the process of their giving.

Give sincerely! False flattery will beget the same from others, and condescending compliments will not do much to raise your present mood.

Bring to Others a Joyful Attitude

Know that the only part of you that is real is the part that experiences joy; all else are lies built upon an illusion. Seek always to have a joyful attitude that comes with finding the beauty in everything you experience. But only when life becomes fully a shared experience with God can true joy be yours. Pursue that oneness as a drowning man seeks air, and once finding it, expands gratefully his lungs with the full consent of his whole mind and body and spirit.

So let the conviction of your will and strength of your desire overcome all obstacles. Learn to desire God's presence more than the food you eat, and soon all excesses will vanish. Love God until you cannot bear but share Him, and all selfishness will likewise be overcome.

And when you come upon a new toy that might delight your children, is not your pleasure great in presenting it to them? How much greater, then, is the pleasure of God in pleasing you, for His love for you is far greater than you can conceive.

So practice in every encounter the bringing of God's message to His beloved. Then even if you are met with indifference, anger, or scorn, He will be well-pleased with you, for even the seed planted upon dry soil and seemingly lost, may one day take root when the rains finally come.

Use Giving As a Way of Receiving

In the giving and receiving of help are the answers to all My secrets. But there are those who are always making a show of giving who have never learned how to give. And there are those who receive but with reluctance and misgivings, so that their receiving is as a burden to them.

But true giving is the giving of Self for the pure joy of the expression of Self. Any other hope for gain is paltry in comparison, and detracts from the joy of Being. Be not afraid to be divinely Self-ish, to seek ever the joy of expression of Self in giving. And the more one gives without hope of other gain, the more one has, for giving enriches the giver.

And those that know not the meaning of giving, can never receive in their hearts, but rather withhold their joy and gratitude as if thereby to diminish their debt.

But the true child of God is loved because of his joy in acceptance and appreciation of all things. And in his heart there shines a light that communicates with the joy of the Giver. And, thus, all joy comes from giving and receiving: is this not My greatest secret?

Accept Your Role in
Controversial Situaltions

Remember that there is a lesson to be learned in all controversial situations which cannot be learned by fighting back in a self-righteous manner. Never fight back, for one cannot fight without inflicting wounds, the sting of which only quickens the tongues of your enemies. Notice that you are not without fault in helping to promote the present calamity that has befallen you. Anger, in part, is an attempt to alleviate oneself of guilt and responsibility.

Disappointment, anxiety, and self-righteous anger have repeatedly been your lot whenever you have expected unusual understanding from those whom you have set up as authority figures. Reflect upon the past and see whether this is not true. Your man-made gods have repeatedly crumbled upon you.

In setting them up, you were attempting to abnegate your own responsibility to be the man or woman you are, and must be, in order to fulfill the expectations that were designed for you in this lifetime. Then, too, consider for a painful moment, whether you have been guilty of putting others into the same dilemma you now find yourself? Notice how invectives cycle like a boomerang.

The situation now clearly calls not for an angry tongue but for a penitent mind and much self-reflection upon the weaknesses that have opened the doors to your present stress.

Be Firm Rather Than Self-Righteous

Self-righteousness is born of envy, guilt and insecurity. Firmness comes from steadfastness of purpose and the entertaining of what is in one's heart, all the while holding the door open to the possibility of being wrong or ill-advised. Self-righteousness brooks no disagreement and entertains no possibility of an alternative course. The man who is firm to what he holds dear with sincerity, humility, and charity suffers no disgrace when found mistaken, and is never lacking friends to console or support him. The self-righteous man suffers disgrace when found wrong, and is surrounded by enemies ready to rejoice in his humiliation.

Test always the heart. A self-righteous attitude stirs the bodily fluids into a tempest of erratic behavior, whereas a firm attitude is maintained in utter calmness, and portrays friendliness and understanding in its expression. The intent is to guide, or help, or increase understanding in those who need this firmness of opinion to strengthen their own shaky purposes.

The self-righteous man always betrays his ego needs, and speaks to maintain or increase his own survival, striving not to increase understanding but to suppress opposition. Learn to listen more. No man who listens well can easily fall into the trap of self-righteousness.

Never Envy The Role of Others

Do not be envious of those with special talents or the faculty of psychic powers. All will be given to you according to your need. Learn never to compare, for each is given his own unique destiny in My plan, to play his own particular role in the furthering of the advancement of all. Accept graciously your part in My cast. The performance of a supporting character is often the most applauded. And all may learn, from taking part, the roles of the others and the important theme of the Play from whichever perspective he participates.

Every man has a unique destiny that makes him special in his relationship to God. If you could see the entirety of the drama being enacted in even the humblest or least of your fellow man you would be moved to bow before him with tears. And the secret is to become a good supporting actor. The tragic figure is most often the one that holds the center of the stage.

God's heart is closest to His supporting cast who take part in the evolving drama of many, rather than with him who is preoccupied with his own role. This will provide a guideline for your behavior toward your fellow man: Try not to dominate the center of the stage, but rather seek to contribute to the development of the roles of your fellow actors in the play. How exciting it is to contemplate this shift in focus from oneself to another.

Avoid Rehearsing Arguments
In Your Head

Notice how time spent in a soliloquy within yourself can destructively detract from time that might best be spent in quiet listening? The argumentative mind is not a contemplative mind. Yet you think it necessary to go through this very time-absorbing process in order to resolve within yourself a petty squabble with a peer.

Again, what is really resolved by this? It serves only to strengthen a self-righteous stance on a position that originally had only a very shaky defense. You foment and increase your irritability and uncharitable attitudes toward an erstwhile friend, which makes it all the more difficult to deal reasonably with him.

Far better, pray for right thinking, free from ego-self. Where negative emotions attach themselves, the ego thrives. Rather, contemplate objectively your true feelings on the matter, maintaining the position most compatible to the image of your Ideal, free from ego-self. No soliloquy is ever needed here.

Part V

The true nature of the battle within is now revealed. Man must develop and exercise his will in overcoming the seduction of his animal nature and to make the important choice between the false ego and the companionship of God. To man alone is given the choice of going his own way or attuning himself willingly to the universal harmony of all things.

The Triune Nature Of Man

Within each human being, resides all strength, all peace, all knowledge, and the means of attuning one with the other. Humans have been gifted by God with an awareness that is their "knowing." It is an awareness that defies analysis and definition, for to define it is to limit it. It is uniquely one's own, and not to be limited in any way by any other being. It has no boundaries and yet is ever growing. Within it resides the center of one's being, the focal point of one's will, and the very universe itself. And no person need ever be envious of another, save as they limit themselves and define another as superior. All that one could want is within.

And everyone has an Intellect, a surface mind if you will, which observes the world or plane one would travel. And if one judges or surmises prematurely one will see one-sided what one has predicted will be there. Thus as each judges so it is; what each seeks each will find; what each fears each creates and then there is no end to each one's discontent.

But rather look for the truth that is there, God's joyful pageant of awareness growing into light. Rather than judge harshly the child who stumbles, the parent who is neglectful, and friend who deceives, see all as at different stages of continuous growth much as the sprouts and the buds and flowers of a giant nursery. Each will add color in its own season. And each, in its every stage of growth, is a joy to the patient botanist who knows the plan of each seed.

But humans, in their ignorance, refuse to watch with patience and appreciation, and would attempt to change everything about them according to their own idea, and thus disharmony within and without occurs leading to much unnecessary suffering for all.

Then too, every person has a center for appreciation through Emotion that is unique to the world of flesh. Emotions add a special color or vitality to perceptions, the desire for which drew man, initially, to the plane of earth. But here, too, one errs in believing that all to be enjoyed must be possessed or consumed. For how can one hope to possess a fraction of what one is capable of enjoying? Rather, every desire can be satisfied within and savored as a special element of the life flow. A flower does not need to be picked to be enjoyed.

The Lower Self is the animal nature and as such contains the instincts for survival common to all beasts, and especially fear, for paralysis or flight, and rage for attack. But while the animals are under the protection of their group spirit and so do not experience their emotions needlessly, humans stand alone, answerable only to themselves and, in this, they perpetuate their fear and anger constantly so that all activity becomes motivated by one or the other. And see what a hell man has wrought for himself upon the earth, requiring frequently the intercession of the Ascended Masters lest he destroy himself. And, thus, in the average person there is not the joy of even the most helpless creature of the forest.

People seek continually new experiences of their own creation and become a victim of their own unbridled imagination, which is the vehicle for their creative powers. Thus they create their own causes for fear and rage whereas, in reality, these emotions are totally unnecessary for survival. Humans, unlike the animal creatures of the earth, can create what environment they choose. In so doing one then becomes desperately preoccupied with fighting against or running from what one has created. In the interim one seeks not joy but satiation, laying waste what one devours, and diminishing one's sensitivity to beauty and to life itself.

Only by consciously diverting one's creative and restless nature from sense pleasures to higher awareness can all men become free to resonate harmoniously with the universe.

Seek God's Presence Within

To all intents and purposes you are the sum composite of your state of mind at any given time. Yet within you is the "I AM" beyond the mind, which, when contacted, can teach you to control the mind. Then you will discover that you, in fact, are not the mind, but the I AM, Himself.

He is I, your Lord, who speaks to you now, and whenever you are receptive to listen. The more strongly you recognize My ever-present Being within, the more strongly is My presence known.

Reaching Me through constant prayer is good, but for your prayers to be answered quickly, you must ask with the full knowledge, faith, and conviction that you have within yourself all power to bring about that which you truly desire.

Know your true desires, and be a partner with Me in carrying them to fruition. Neither will this require an attitude of stubbornness or defiance which man is so prone to adopt.

Desire Me, and according to the purity of your desire you shall know Me. Seek Me and soon you will see Me in every tangible perception as well as every perception intangible. These are all reflections of your own thinking, and inasmuch as I Am the source of all thought, all things capable of your reflection are reflections of Me.

Keep open to Me by keeping yourself always in a loving frame of mind, and do willingly and gratefully that which has been set before you to do.

All emotion, all feeling, all desire, and all consciousness is but a manifestation of different aspects of My Being. Yet know that your being is one with My Being. Notice that I do not ask you to understand, but simply to know this! People are so enamored of their Intellects that it serves as a block to knowing Me. But all knowing is knowing Me!

Experience Me from the depths of your being as an innocent child. Refrain from worshiping those things that are but reflections of Me, or you will be caught in the trap of your own illusions.

Because people tire so easily from repetition, I must constantly change the face of truth. Know that all truth is everywhere to be found. I have encapsulated all of it in everything I have created. Never be sure you know anything from a single glance. There is far more than you can ever know in even a speck of dust, and far more wisdom in every passage of inspired writing than you can ever understand.

Approach Me, then, with humility and I will embrace you as my Own.

The Nature of the Ego

Much confusion has arisen in recent years over the concept of the ego. The ego is that necessary unifying force which gives direction to all intent. It is not intent itself. All life has ego, and when the ego is fed with lies it proceeds without judgment accordingly. The ego merely carries out your orders to determine your behavior in the world. It is fed, like a computer, your accepted self-image, your imagined needs and fears, your conclusions from all past experiences, and whatever other limitations or beliefs you wish to give it. (No wonder it is so often anxious and over-whelmed!) It then proceeds as best it can, under the circumstances, to allow for the greatest protection of the self-system.

It is your will which decides the direction your ego will go. Your will, which determines the course of its input, and then imbues it with intent out of your hidden desires.

Make more conscious, then, your motives and be more aware of the image you feed your ego, so that it can be relieved of the burden of deception. You tell yourself a lie, and then waste untold energy trying to lie to others about the lie.

What is the Truth? Look constantly to the Source of Truth, and covet Truth more dearly than yourself. Let the Truth ring out from every body organ and every muscle fiber. Then will all energy you now use to protect the lie be made available to the Self within.

How To Escape the Influence of the Ego

Stop thinking! Your thoughts are idle and the work of the ego, which prevents you from listening. And what is there to think about when everything is already in God's hands? He has designed an ingenious play in which you may work out your salvation through participation in it. You have only to let go and let the various elements play out their parts.

You need only to feel gratitude and praise and listen attentively for your cues. See everyone and everything as serving you to this purpose. That which creates fear, apprehension, and desire interferes with the Divine Plan.

Thinking is a device of the ego that diverts, restricts, or blocks awareness away from a sense of oneness. Out of thinking fear arises, and out of thinking alternative goals contrary to God's purpose arise. As one grows older, his mind tends to become progressively more clogged with thoughts.

Let go of thought, and along with this all personal motive and all personal desire. Observe without question, be attentive without thought, and soon the proper perspective needed will be reached.

God's Love Overcomes Fear

Fear is a natural reaction to the illusions of the ego. The ego first makes you vulnerable and then paints horrible possibilities which, often, eventually become a reality. And notice how the ego uses fear to make you dependent upon it. In your meditations it promotes resistance by interposing a harsh and punitive god between Me and you. And how difficult it is to distract your thoughts from the preoccupation with the fears it creates to leave your mind open to My input.

And then you find it easier to seek outside for sources of help. And the more you persist in this, the less you will turn to Me and the greater becomes your fear and insecurity despite the quality of advice being offered. And, although I may speak to you from every new acquaintance you make, so long as you see Me as outside of yourself, then there will be fear.

But let yourself be vulnerable to your fear that it might be exposed as a tool of the ego. See your fear as the ego's only possible offering to you and then, with humility, invite Me to be your guest. See Me as all that which, even in your greatest despair, would bring your heart to leap with joy.

See Me as sitting here in a perpetual state of Buddhic peace, inviting you to join Me. Begin to yearn to see the world through My eyes, and then you will be able to behold the face of love everywhere. And where there is love, there is no place for fear.

How We Swerve From the Path

Man is vain and self-indulgent. Even in his most selfless acts of sacrifice, or demonstrations of piety, he seeks secretly in his heart to serve himself, to further his personal cause and to gratify his false ego.

Man seeks to take from others what he, himself, cannot give; while serving God is possible only through giving. Therefore, all that you desire—praise, acceptance, adulation and love, give first to God, that you might receive them.

Man is ever self-indulgent, making every excuse to satisfy his whims or sensual pleasures against all reason of his inner conscience. Each moment ask yourself, "Is this necessary for the greater development of my soul or the building of my body temple?"

And then consider with sober mind how many precious moments of your day are lost in idle fantasy, how many opportunities for growth neglected, how much harm through self indulgence you have inflicted upon yourself. In little things, in little ways, according to the pattern which is formed through practice, do you grow or die.

Then, too, man identifies himself with whatever cause or material thing the false ego chooses to make real. Thus, friendships may be broken or several days spent in misery over the loss of a card game or a sporting contest.

Let not the playthings of the earth divert you from your knowing Me; and yet there is nothing either real or imagined in which you cannot find Me if you look.

> A tense mind reciting mantras
>
> Is a tense mind reciting mantras.
>
> And when it has finished reciting,
>
> It is a tense mind that has finished reciting mantras.
>
> But a mind calmed by the will
>
> Is a calm mind responsive to the will,
>
> And becomes one with the mantra it recites.

And why should the mind be tense when the truth is so beautiful? In the greatest discomfort, apprehension, and pain, let the mind be joyful in the thought that the unending truth is beautiful beyond description.

Learn to know the power of the mind when reined by an iron will.

The Lie of False Personality

When one has indeed actualized a happy marriage between the child of emotion and the intellect of will, then the cleansing of the temple may begin in earnest. Then all negativities, all anger, all jealousy, all hate is slowly consumed in the fires of love.

See, then, your present personality as only a hypothetical possibility, just as ignorance, unawareness of God, and negative emotions against self and others, which make of life a hell, are all merely theoretical possibilities that you, yourself, have chosen to experience and to overcome. Thus the Truth, when known, dissolves it all and makes you free.

To know the Truth you must resist, at every turn, the Lie that says that Evil is and God is not. The Lie that make illusion real says that you have needs that need to be fed from without, for within yourself is all love, all fulfillment, all peace, and all Truth that can be known. So as your temple is cleansed of the lie that breeds greed and avarice, let it be filled with the Truth that gives, instead of takes, and which emanates good in all directions.

The flow is ever outward, for that which is received from outside deceives. Thus, let Light fill the temple and let loving be your joy. And if any love you, let that be their joy. And the flame that bravely flickers now amidst the tempest of the world will one day brighten the skies and bring an end to the storm.

The Development of the Will

The will and the power of the will can only be known through the continual exercise and manifesting of it in all manners of situations. Know that your will is you! And inasmuch as it is you, it is Me also. As the proper attunement of a sound can ring a distant bell or shatter a glass, so the proper attunement of your will through daily exercise will soon awaken the sleeping centers of power within and shatter the illusion of the world.

Yet there is always the battle within against which the will must be strengthened. Thus, acknowledge and accept this struggle of the will against the false ego, and be not dismayed when you occasionally succumb to temptations, moods of anger, or the trap of procrastination. But be constantly aware of the battle, knowing that its strength must always equal yours, else no development is possible.

Thus you will win and lose, each time strengthened by your winning, but rarely hurt by the losing unless you succumb in shame and despair, rather than immediately arising anew with increased determination. But remember the path of great danger and needless suffering is trod by those who willfully succumb to the false ego, thereby increasing its power and diminishing theirs. Give nothing to the false ego without your greatest struggle! Even then you must occasionally lose, lest complacency intoxicate you.

The Raising of Consciousness

The raising of consciousness is the ultimate goal of man, and the ability to do this infinitely is his birthright. The expanding of your Consciousness is your only worthwhile goal. There is no ego in this. It is a divine selfishness, the fulfilling of a divine desire, and must be sought after as avidly as a man who is held against his will under water seeks air. Those who are fearful, lest this raise also the ego, are not understanding of the process and are feeding the ego by their entanglement with it.

Each level of consciousness is a new dimension which cannot be understood or comprehended by the level below. God is progressively known at higher and higher levels of Truth, Beauty and Love that cannot be described in words. See how the preoccupation with self and its petty concerns limits your consciousness.

The expansion of consciousness can only take place in the eternal Now, and the process must be constant to be effective. Thus, your preoccupation with the past and worry about the future can stop or reverse the process. The ego would keep you underwater, preoccupied with the fish and trying to compete with them. But, wherever you are, keep thirsting for the highest level with all of your heart and mind.

Everything You Experience
Originates From Within

All things must be seen as originating from within. Look without and then learn to examine your reactions independently within. Later you will be able to do this in the reverse order. As a child, did not your heart and body respond as one to the singing birds and the morning sun as if within they struck a vibrant cord? But even this has now been closed off by your constant pressured considerations of other things.

If you wish your heart to open, then will it to do so. If then it does not open, only two possibilities exist: either you do not truly, without ambivalence or equivocation, wish it to open, or else your heart does not believe you.

You must know your own will, and then work to convince your body that you are entirely sincere in your new attitudes and insist upon being obeyed. And how well is your body disciplined to obey your will? Inconsistency of discipline will spoil even the most adaptive child.

And unless you have respect for your own words, how can you expect them to consistently move others? Say only what you believe, and then let it come from the heart. It is well that you do not consider yourself as important, but see to it that what you do is important and especially that which is done in My name. Then let your motives be all for Me, and take courage from the thought of serving Me.

Live Each Day As If It
Were Your Last

Live this day, and every day, as if it were your only and your last. Be never mindful of what has past or what might be, but concentrate all awareness upon the task at hand. Do not be afraid that you are unprepared; honest effort will always bring the desired or the needed results. One day lived fully like this could free you from your present entanglement in seemingly overwhelming obligations.

Make a beginning today to give this a try. Those things that must be done of the moment will be given. See to it that your will is not distracted or fall prey to idle considerations that hamper it. This does not mean that every moment must be spent productively in man's terms, but much time must be spent in giving, which as yet you cannot see as productive to yourself. Rather, you must develop the attitude of seeing all activity as one of giving. Your present conflicts and anxieties are the result of working too hard for gain.

And the more you receive, either in wages or in praise, the more your life becomes a drudgery. There can never be enough in the receiving of these. Envy no man who seemingly is superior to yourself in obtaining these. But let your pleasures be in the giving, expecting no other gain that this. And, thus, the poor with hardly a penny to spare can attain the pleasures of the rich.

Time and Its Proper Use

Time has been given to you as a gift that was meant for your enjoyment. But as with all gifts, misused and misunderstood it may become a burden. Man suffers from the twin complaints of not having enough time and of having too much time. And there is the unhappiness and guilt that comes with the wasting of it. For man's approach to it is not unlike his attitude toward all of his earthly treasures: He would save it and hoard it, bargain for it, resent the sharing of it, while craving more of it and limiting himself to his own imagined possession of it, all the while seeking desperately in vain to enjoy it.

And what is the lesson that is here to be learned in all of this? Namely, this, that nothing of earthly treasures can be stored up to a day of better use. All of their value rests upon the use that is made of them in the fleeting moment when they are first presented to you. And the spending of them in this moment determines what will be made available to you in the next.

And so with time, the opportunity missed is never recovered. The letter that must be answered today will never be the same tomorrow. The kind word, the friendly gesture, the simple pleasures of the moment slip quickly by and can never be recovered. So make use of what you have *now* and never worry about tomorrow.

Everything is in a Constant State of Change

All development progresses in cycles: when one is completed, another automatically begins, the former being a natural forerunner of the second. Reflect for a moment upon the cycles of the evolution of ages, of planetary movements, of the seasons, and of the phases of growth of all living things. Everything has its time and place and purpose. And the cycles of the atoms are in harmony with the cycles of the stars. Thus, everything is constantly in a state of flux or change according to a master plan or purpose. And it is change that refreshes and stirs the consciousness of all life. The experience of change awakens your consciousness of being. So expect nothing to be the same twice.

Although everything is influenced by the changes of the seasons and of the stars, man was given free will to choose what attitude he wishes as regards the changes about him. When those attitudes are not in harmony with the natural laws of change then irritability, impatience, and anger result.

Man can hold still while the things about him change, and thus he can learn the patterns of change and the ways of God, but this can only be done to advantage if one has cultivated the proper attitude of mind. For attitude is everything! Man alone is responsible for his attitudes. When you have mastered the mind so as to maintain right attitude you are already in God's kingdom.

Let Your Will Schedule Your Mind

Nothing brings greater control over the mind than the constant focusing of it upon the task at hand. The mind, when working without awareness, is at best a diffuse and evasive servant. At worst, it can usurp your throne and take you upon a not so merry ride.

Make each day, upon awakening, a new start, planning the activities of that day and the apportioning of time necessary to complete what is deemed worthwhile. Practice maintaining yourself strictly to that schedule. When you fail in this, consider whether it was the result of poor planning or of a weak will.

Focus your mind upon that which you have planned, relieving your mind of other worries or considerations. Thus, learn to anticipate and meet the challenges others will make upon your mind's schedule. Remember, there are no excuses—only lessons that need learning. Notice how you are paralyzed by poor planning, letting the pressures of the day determine your activities in a disorganized fashion.

Let not time become your master, against whom you wage a perpetual stubborn battle. Any man might be judged by what use he makes of his time. And in the day-to-day planning and use of time, the will is strengthened.

See Life as a Twice-Told Tale

All of life must be faced as a twice-told tale and all events seen from the perspective of last year's newspaper. Total indifference and detachment helps one to complete the necessary process of earth existence as soon as possible so as to move on—yet not with a solemn face or demeanor of pain or depression, but rather as one going through the motions of a dance as a devotional act to God.

All that must be experienced will be experienced, and so the secret is to experience fully without expectations, to encounter without apprehensions, to accept without regret, to be at home with ambiguity, and to desire nothing.

This is the secret of getting out of oneself and participating in the celebration of life as a companion to God. Let the current flow and let God steer the course. All you need is an open ear and a ready heart.

See all life as a symphony to which you are privy to share in your own box seat beside God. Never question the plot nor doubt God's plan for you. And who are you, but that spark of His essence who would see it all from another perspective.

Space and the Movements
of Man Within It

Time and space was created as a media for the incubation of unconscious spirit until it grows into awareness. Thus man is confined, as in a cocoon, as long as the Christ Consciousness remains asleep, hibernating, as it were, within him. All space is created by thought and hence filled with the energy and seed-atoms of God, no less than the material manifestations within it. The movements of one upon the other create the musical tones of God's symphonic expression. It is a display of light upon light, color upon color, sound upon sound, and matter upon space all in accord with the central Note of creation.

And those who are able to attune their eyes and their ears to the exquisite interplay of awakening spirit are filled with a delight of indescribable ecstasy.

How then, might one proceed to attune himself to the rhythm and the tempo of God? By becoming aware of it, looking and listening for the pattern in every minor experience or occurrence.

But to do this, man must give up his own preconceived ideas and become less attached to the individual "notes" that makes him attempt to cling too long to some while discarding others. God's symphony fills the entire range of the scale, and you must accept it all in order to hear it.

See all space as filled with God consciousness, and the movements of your body within it as creating a harmonic sound sweet to the ear of God. And as your mind is thus focused upon this process, it will gradually become awakened to a full awareness of God. See every movement which you make as important to God. Is this so difficult to imagine? Can you not, for an hour or more, maintain an interest in watching the movements of a few fish in your tropical tank?

How much more, then, are your thoughts and activities of interest to God. His joy is in the gradual spiritual enfoldment of His children into the awareness of Him.

Be aware of God's caring presence in all that you do, and look for the patterns He constantly presents before you that you might awaken to His presence. Let every movement of your body in space and every thought that you transmit be as a sharing with Him. This lesson is so simple, and yet for many so difficult. Practice constantly that you become perfect in its execution.

The Rules For Attainment

The rules for attainment of all that I have are simple, yet often unheeded: The more you listen, the more you will hear. The more you accept, the more you will receive. The more that you give, the more to you that is given. That which is used grows, and that which is neglected dies. Awareness leads to more awareness, happiness brings happiness, and love begets love.

If man would but see himself as a nameless consciousness experiencing Me, then all that he would need to find Me would be given. Man finds what he seeks, and becomes a victim to his own desires. That which is sent forth grows within, and that which is closed off forms a prison.

Let not fear, pride, and hope for selfish gain exile you from the garden of My blessings. Why struggle for that which you already have, or fear that which only your fear creates? The lie makes you fight, but the Truth teaches surrender. Be not afraid to acknowledge your ignorance, for only when you know you are asleep can you awaken.

Raise the Vibration of Your Emotions

Develop your will by increasing the vibration and polarity of every experience given to you. This must be a constant effort in order to become an automatic function of the will. Only then may total control of the mind be attained.

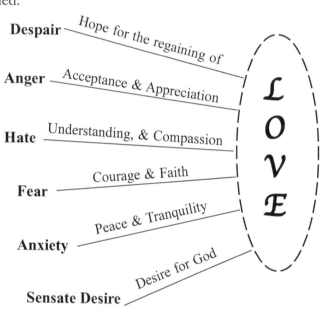

Notice how unwilling the mind always is to leave whatever extreme of polarity it may be entertaining. For the nature of each extreme is to feed upon itself, grasping energy from your will or consent to further intensify or stubbornly maintain its extreme position. In just such a fashion do men create Hell for themselves and then refuse to leave. But Heaven is the mastery of every conceivable experience into the experience of Love.

Focus Your Awareness Upon Love

There is only awareness; Being without perception.

When you came into the world you experienced fear. Out of that fear perceptions were created. These perceptions formed the basis of your reality thereafter.

You are not in touch with your original perceptions because your body defended against them. What you now experience is an illusion elaborated as a defense against a deeper reality which you fear.

You must learn to heal your perceptions by recognizing that the fear behind them is unreal.

You must learn to cultivate the unconditional love space within your heart independent of all external influences.

Then, you may practice choosing, indiscriminately about you, targets to which you have no responsibility or emotional investment attached. You can love a blade of grass or a glass sitting on the table with equal intensity.

Next, you can practice transmuting other forms of love by drawing it into the unconditional love space. Gradually, perceptions will become more and more impersonal. And as they are thus healed, the true essence behind all things will be revealed. This is a natural result of daring to be aware.

In this way, awareness is linked to love.

Seek to Live In Divine Presence

All those who read My words frequently, as I have given them in various Holy Scriptures to different cultures in different ages, will surely find their way into My presence. Devotional love (meditate frequently upon its meaning) is a sure way into My presence.

Devotional love is performed in every activity wherein the mind is acutely aware of My presence while the body moves mechanically, deriving no enjoyment and expecting no reward or fruition from the activity itself.

The mind attuned to Me shall find itself in Me. Attunement to the lower self places one at the mercy of the false ego which leads to unbearable suffering and misery. The neutral point, or procrastination, leads likewise to death.

The quickening of the spiritual energies must be an ever constant process, for the flames grow quickly cold upon this dead earth! Then beware, lest the false flames of lower-self passion be sought as warmth and for satisfaction. The false ego craves earthly gratification, but the true spirit within craves only My love. Know that that which you crave you shall have!

See to it that you are ever attuned to the soft voice of the spirit within.

The Pathos of Mankind

The Pathos of Mankind is a dream from My innermost Being of unconsciousness awakening into Light and of Selfishness developing into Good. It is the story of redemption. It is the joy of reunion that follows loss or separation.

It is the reclaiming of the lost and the transformation of loneliness into joyful communion. It is the separating of My consciousness into individual "beams" that will one day once again be totally reunited within Me.

The barrier is man's free will operating in an illusory world that makes alternative choices to Me appear tempting. It is the saga on a cosmic scale of Love lost and found. Of course, it is not really ever lost, but merely appears so. The secret is to stop looking and just desire it!

But when the heart is hardened and eyes are blinded to the truth, then it is necessary for one to help all and all to help one. For no one can make it of his own, nor can one be saved before all others because each is part of the same beam, and separateness is only an illusion.

Does all this seem so simple to you? When everything appears a thousand times more simple, then you will know that you are not very far from the Truth.

Epilogue

The average reader of this little book will initially see it as merely a collection of inspirational and uplifting thoughts. However, when the full meaning of the words it contains pierces through the veil of the ego, the reality of their Source can elicit a reaction of open-mouthed awe. I, myself, become more transfixed with every new reading of them over the years.

The messages are very clear: The veil between ourselves and God is very thin. But to pierce it we must learn to overcome selfishness, which creates a stubborn hold upon our thoughts and aspirations and that forces us to see ourselves as separate from everything and everyone around us. Selfishness puts us into an endless struggle for survival and, very often, makes life seem impossible. However, regardless of your past or present circumstances, it is never too late to surrender and to put everything into God's hands in order to bring a more fulfilling ending to this story that is your life.

For those who are seriously exploring meditation, I would like to add a few practices that I have found helpful over the years:

Before beginning to meditate, I breathe in from my right nostril for twenty counts, hold my breathe for twenty counts, and exhale through my mouth for twenty counts. Then I breathe into my left nostril for twenty counts, hold my breathe for twenty counts, and then exhale through my right nostril for twenty counts. Next I have a glass of water with the juice of half a lemon in it. I drink slowly, as I recite healing affirmations for my body.

1

When you have been able to attain a sense of no-thinking within your head, practice maintaining it after opening your eyes.

2

Be aware of being aware without thinking. Try to do this while engaged in routine chores.

3

Next envision God being aware of your being aware. Gradually you will develop the sense of God seeing through your eyes.

4

Then observe whatever comes to your five senses and try to experience this as an attempt to awaken you to a higher level of awareness. It is in this way that you might experience what is called, in Zen Buddhism, a "satori." An indescribable feeling may come from noticing something as seemingly insignificant as the ticking of a clock or the angle of a shadow from the leg of a kitchen chair.

Still, it is very difficult to live between two worlds. I would like to share a very personal experience. In the late 1970's, I was the medical director of the George Miller Jr. Center for Multi-handicapped Children and Adults in Northern California. There was always a struggle, as today, for adequate funding of mental health programs, and I had a strong distaste for the politics involved.

On the day that a meeting was scheduled in my large conference room, I felt the need to meditate before the arrival of the heads of the various agencies that were competing for County funds. I later recorded my experience:

How easy it all seems when I am in the consciousness of knowing. I say to myself, "Why cannot other men make this simple shift of putting everything into Your hands and seeing the world through Your eyes. It has everything to commend it, a feeling of joy and freedom from fear. Then in every tree or form of life I see, I sense Your personal presence. All the world is my playground in which You are preparing every moment for me to enjoy, to learn, and to gather experiences that will lead to my ultimate awakening.

It is as if we are in a dream together, and my awakening from it is dependent upon my willingness to be aware of the clues all about. You are there, ever prodding me to higher and higher levels of consciousness. And this feeling is increased as I get more and more out of myself and let Your consciousness flow through me through my accepting, my selfless giving, and my praying for others.

Then there is no separation between us and the joy and love in my heart feeds the bliss in my spine. While acutely conscious of everything around me, I am aware that the only thing that matters is what is going on inside. And there is so much happening right now, that there is no concern for the future. And when I pray, it s as if it is to myself, and it has the quality not so much of a supplication as a So be it. And all of the saints are my friends bestowing Their blessings, and I know that Their hearts could never entertain anger, jealousy, or criticism, but only love.

How easy , I think, it is to maintain this feeling forever. I can do nothing but grow.

And, then, my reverie is interrupted by the impatience of a colleague whose anxieties and irritability toward me shift me into a feeling of defensive self-consciousness. And now the ego is in charge once more, and acutely aware that what is going on out there is what really matters. Now, full of righteous indignation, I enter the conference room, prepared to force my own ideas upon others who are threatening my future plans.

And, suddenly, I realize that the magic is gone. And the shift that had seemed so easy is now impossible to make. How long must I wait to again find the handle to the door?

It helps to see God and the high teachers as loving Beings with a sense of humor, but who are not reluctant to admonish you when you persist along the wrong path. I must include an example here. At one time, when beginning to meditate, I stated in a somewhat brash but playful mood: "Jesus, I want You to know that God loves every one of his creations equally, which means that He loves me just as much as he loves You despite all of your pain and suffering for us."

And, then, I was struck by the following thought that resounded in my head: *That is very true. The only difference between you and Me is that I love Him more!*

———————————

Try to see God as your Lover, Brother, caring Father, nurturing Mother, and Friend all in one. The first thing that God will do is to help you to accept His love, to feel worthy, and to forgive the past which now fills your head with knots of anger, regret, unforgiveness, and blame. Think of Him as reaching out to address you in the following way:

Forgive the past. It was all My doing. I allowed you to be exposed to pain, grief, abuse, embarrassment, failures, and even anguish in order to get you to where you are right now—turning to Me as your only source of hope.

If you knew how much I loved you, you would forgive Me. If you allowed yourself to feel My love, you would never regret anything that "might have been" or anything that you lost or wanted and couldn't have in the past. I understand everything you have been through because I experienced it with you, and love you for all of it.

I allowed you to be lost because I wanted you to experience the joy of finding Me. There is nothing you have to do or to become in order to be perfect in My eyes, just as I created you. Do not underestimate the gift of consciousness that I gave to you. It is presently like a small seed that has the potential to grow to infinity and beyond, until you become as a real companion and an equal to Me.

I am putting you through experiences that force you to keep growing. I am always guiding you, but it is you who must be willing to take advantage of the opportunities and the challenges I place before you. In participating actively in your own growth, you will develop and enjoy your own sense of uniqueness while still being one with Me.

The journey is not easy and sometimes very painful but, in the end, you would not have wanted it any other way. Yet, there is always the availability of a resting place if you will learn to enter into the silence and invite Me to help you to experience, for one brief holy instant, the joy of your Divinity.

Glossary

Christ Consciousness: This is a generic term, accepted by even many non-Christian religions, for a state of total realization of Self and of one's relationship to the All. It is a state of no resistance, of total surrender, of perfect attunement with the divine intent of the Universal All until one becomes essentially indistinguishable from It.

Ego: The ego represents the sum totality of one's identity, and beliefs, at any given moment in time. It changes as one's concept of himself changes. Man's ego functions to perpetuate the survival of the physical body and of his belief system. (Either one may take priority over the other, depending upon the circumstances). The false ego isolates man from his fellowman and makes him unbelievably selfish and often cruel in his dealings with others. The false ego seals off the heart. It may give lip-service to God but, in reality denies His presence. When the intellect become motivated by power, and allows the passions of the lower self to assume a sadistic quality, then the false ego becomes truly demonic. The false ego is sometimes referred to as Satan, the father of lies, in the Bible.

Personality: This comprises the constellation of mechanical patterns, reflex emotions, survival reactions, and invested drives toward contrived goals and imaginary needs that we have come to identify with as our self. It is our outer Persona, quite separate from out Inner Being. As such, is assumes our given name which we then feel compelled to promote and defend, often at great cost to our personal energy.

Holy Spirit:
The voice of God that speaks to man.

Intellect: This is the surface consciousness that integrates our perceptions, makes associations, and orients our awareness to fit the 3-dimensional world. Problems arise when it begins to make judgments and assumptions based upon preconceived expectations arising out of the prejudices and false belief systems handed down by our parents and society. Worse, the Intellect becomes impatient in its role of observer and seeks to become the doer. This presumptuous decision is made to feel necessary by a closing off and denial of the true Source of all things. Then man's troubles really begin as he is filled with constant anxiety and a sense of overwhelm at the obvious impossibility of the task.

The Full Mind: This is more than the intellect alone. The higher abstract mind can transcend most of the well-recognized limitations of the lower and often judgemental mind. The abstract mind is capable of true intuition and tapping the wisdom of spirit as well as dealing directly with the power and creative essence of divine archetypes.

The Lower Mind: This is the coordinator of the five senses, activities of the physical body and the organs of excretion and sex. It seeks fullfillment in the external world. It looks for satisfaction and sensual pleasure with relatively little concern for consequences.

Self: (Higher Self): This is our true Identity, independent of a physical body, our transcendental Beingness in atonement with God.

Self: (lower self): This is the animal consciousness that we have possessed and that now possesses us. It is not basically evil, but because it has been programmed from generation to generation with fear, prejudice, and hate it can be rightfully referred to as "the demon within". It is naturally selfish in all of its aims and it seeks sense gratification with almost no consideration of consequences. Its urges, when strong, are almost impossible to resist without outside help. It operates through the imagination to tax the will. Our own current identity is associated with this animal self, and in man's present stage of evolution, a strong social structure is needed to keep it leashed.

Soul: The individualized spirit that comes into existence when the universal " I" first conceives this particular expression of Itself.

Will: Just as every level of consciousness has its ego counterpart, so the decision-making mechanism determining the activity at each level constitutes its will. Thus, there is an awareness that has intent in the lower self, and a mechanism of intent or will in the Intellect as well as in one's Higher Self. Ultimately, all of the lower wills must voluntarily subordinate or harmonize themselves totally to the will of the Higher Self that is at one with the will of God.

Witness: Before any real development can take place, it is mandatory that we establish a sense of awareness independent of the intellect, self, and ego which is able to stand off and observe impartially the charade played out by our own behavior. It is this witness that is addressed by the Higher Self in meditation and exhorted to work constantly toward freeing oneself from the false ego.

With help, this Witness is able to progressively overcome the tugging of the lower self and the phantom fears of the Intellect and draw all awareness into itself. Through this process our awareness may grow to a gradual or sudden rebirth into Christ Consciousness.